What people are saying about...
Dammit, I Love You

"These stories are all about love, all kinds of love, the givers and takers, the objects of love. But no two are alike. They're stories about mothers, a brother, a man or a woman, a boy, and some girls, a bottle of gin. Hearts are lent and forgiven, broken and lost. This collection's a songbook, love's stories retold, hard to put down, close to the heart."

— *Ellen McNeal*
Author of Taking on Water,
Weaver, Editor for The Comstock Review

"This notable collection of fifteen stories of love is as varied in tone and taste as the individually wrapped candies in a Valentine's gift box. Some are hard and tough, others soft and chewy, still others salty and bitter that go down hard while packing a punch. This is a remarkable set where for every reader there's a gem or two to start the taste buds salivating."

— *Howard Jay Smith,*
Author of Beethoven in Love: Opus 139 *and*
Opening the Doors to Hollywood

"These candid glimpses into the lives of fifteen ordinary people with extraordinarily loving hearts leaves the reader longing to know more about each character. This smorgasbord of enticing, varied and dramatic stories inspires us to always summon the courage to love unconditionally."

— *Debra Metelits,*
Author of Wise Older Woman: Growing in Grace and Sass

BRANDT
STREET
PRESS

Dammit, I Love You

Editors: Scott Smith and Anita Kulina

© 2016 by Brandt Street Press

Published by
Brandt Street Press
5885 Bartlett Street
Pittsburgh, PA 15217
www.brandtstreetpress.com

ISBN: 978-0-9742607-5-4
Library of Congress Control Number: 2015956670

Cover and Book Design by
Mike Murray
Pearhouse Productions
Pittsburgh, PA
www.pearhouse.com

Printed in the United States of America

LOVE SWINGS by Judy Jones   5
*A girl's persistent fantasies force her to face
an awful truth*

YOUNG, *YOUNG* LADIES by Will Link   21
If he's 34 and she's 21, does that matter? Yes.

WELCOME BACK, RICHARD,   31
TO THE CROWN AND ANCHOR by Deborah Ross
*An imaginary conversation challenges a woman
to rethink her choices*

CONFESSIONS OF MY DYING FATHER   41
by Stevie Leigh
Listening is hard, but it's worth the pain

DISSOLVE by Amanda Roskos   53
*The hole in her heart was filled by the
person she least expected*

WHAT HAPPENED WITH JACOB by Brent C Dill   73
*No one wants to call 911 and say the words
"domestic dispute"*

FORTY-FIFTH REUNION by Susan Martin   91
It's not the one she had anticipated

MERCY by Michael Moran   105
He knows she might kill him but he can't stay away

THE INVITATION by Jodi Teti   119
The tribulations of being 13 can linger for a lifetime

BUT WOULD YOU FIGHT WITH ME   133
FOREVER? by Lisa L. Kirchner
The saving grace of arguments

SO WHAT IS UNCONDITIONAL LOVE   143
ANYWAY? by Bari Benjamin
Being a mother is not all hearts and roses

PATRICIA by Richard Zielinski   155
A boy, a girl, and the death of innocence

THE OKAYEST BROTHER by Ellen E. Hyatt   167
Why do three little words mean so much?

384 DAYS by Megan Arnold   177
The anatomy of a crush

SAFE DUTY ASSIGNMENT by Thomas Johnson   191
Love and loss in wartime Vietnam

A NOTE TO THE READER

Love can hurt. We all know that. Whether the love has been a parent, a child, a lover, a friend, we've all walked into a situation with stars in our eyes and left with a black eye instead.

The 15 courageous people in this book share those stories. They remind us of what it feels like to hurt, but they also remind us of the strength those scars can foster. Being torn apart can be the one thing that makes us whole.

The stories in this book are true, though names were sometimes changed to protect the guilty.

Love might change us, but it will never weaken us. We are always stronger, dammit, because we love.

— Scott Smith & Anita Kulina,
Editors

LOVE SWINGS

Judy Jones

PATSY SWUNG THE ARM OF THE 45 record player one more time on "Don't Be Cruel," her favorite song. We joined Elvis at the top of our lungs.

"My turn now!" I carefully set on my favorite record, "Heartbreak Hotel."

"Have you ever noticed," asked Patsy, "that my favorite song is about the beginning of love and yours is about breaking up?"

"Oh, don't be so cruel, Patsy," I sang.

Patsy was staying the weekend with my family and me. We often tried to arrange being together on weekends. She lived in town and had to take the bus home with me on Friday, but then my mother would have to drive her home on Sunday night. We stayed up late planning our futures, thinking about getting engaged to handsome boys. We never actually reached the altar in our fantasies, or those boys who waited for us in cummerbunds that matched our color schemes, but we planned in great detail our wedding gowns and the dresses of our bridesmaids, our multi-tiered wedding cakes and the ever-changing themes and colors of our weddings. Patsy's favorite color this year was blue and mine was lavender. She wanted her gown to be a long, clingy ivory silk one, while I wanted a stark white billowing skirt of tulle netting over millions of lace petticoats. Love would be beautiful for us, never cruel.

That love could be cruel was something Patsy and I had witnessed mostly at the movies or in books. We knew there was real-life cruelty because we both came from families that divorced and remarried, and, in Patsy's case, divorced again. My father left our family when I was eight. I missed him terribly and had seen him only three times in the ensuing years. My father followed the custom of the day, becoming one of the men who left and made new homes for themselves. I missed his laughter, his joy of living and the pictures he would often take of me. He photographed me running home from school, playing jacks with friends, or dressed up in Mother's clothes, all bejeweled and posing. A whole life of memories and thwarted plans fell away from me like drops of water when the shower is turned off.

I was 13 when my mother remarried. The wedding was in late spring. She married a farmer and they had to get the wedding in before the season really took hold.

The farmer, my stepfather, was as exacting in his daily habits as he was in his farming. All the rows had to be straight, all fences neatly aligned. Mother and I kept busy that first summer learning how to be good—a good wife and stepdaughter—running to town if my stepfather needed anything to fix machinery, and keeping to his farmer's schedule. Breakfast was after the milking was done and the cows put out to pasture, and dinner had to be on the table by 12 noon. He always said "12 noon," something Patsy and I mocked and laughed about when we were alone. Supper followed the evening milking at 6:30.

Dinner was the most important, and biggest, meal of the day. When my stepfather and his hands came in from the fields, they washed up at the pump in the backyard. Everything had to be on the table and ready to go. He wanted fresh vegetables with his meals, always a plate of green onions and radishes with salt and, his favorite, a plate of sliced tomatoes. Mother's vegetable garden the first summer of her marriage was a challenge for her. The radishes were too hot, the green onions too lanky and the tomato skins too tough.

One day, after we washed up the breakfast dishes, Mother said, "Let's go over to Mrs. Langfeld's place." I didn't know who Mrs. Langfeld was, but I hopped into the truck beside Mother and we drove about a mile toward town. When she pulled into the lane of an old house, I saw why we had come. On a towel under one of the trees was a sign that said, "Tomatoes 5 cents. Better ones are 10." Mother looked over the tomatoes and picked out the firm ones and put the soft ones back. Mrs. Langfeld came and Mother paid her sixty cents. The two of them chatted about tomatoes and the weather, about when to pull radishes so they weren't too hot. I heard laughter from the side of the house. Two older high school girls sat on swings that hung from a tree. I'd never met them, but I knew them instantly. They were the sisters, Dallas and Tennessee. I figured out we must be at their grandmother's house. At the high school, they had reputations as girls headed for trouble. Everybody talked about them, and about their father, too, how he'd named them for places he'd rather be. He was a dog runner, capturing dogs and sending them by train to someplace in the south that did experiments on them. People said he wasn't above taking dogs right off a farm while a family was away. My stepfather always put Old Suze, his Border collie, in the barn when we weren't home.

I watched the girls swing back and forth. Their summer dresses of light cotton were lovely, and when they swung high into the air, their skirts billowed over their thighs. I couldn't stop looking at them. When they grew tired of pumping themselves up high, they spun circles between them, catching the rope on each other's swings, looking my way and laughing. Their smiles, outlined in bright red lipstick, were big. Neither wore stockings, showing off the sophistication of their clean-shaven legs. Three days after we bought Mrs. Langfeld's tomatoes, Dallas would climb out of a bedroom window using a sheet that Tennessee wrapped around a bedstead. She'd slide down as far as she could before falling into the arms of an older man who would whisk her away. He was a widower whose first wife had died by drowning, leaving him with four small children.

This event was the talk of the town. Mother used it to lecture me about sex and the mistakes girls make when pressured by boys.

"They probably had sex. She was probably pregnant. I'm quite sure of it," Mother said as we sat in the truck at the edge of the field waiting for my stepfather to finish spraying for weeds in the beans. I hated these talks. They seemed tawdry. Even the word "sex" felt dirty.

"Think of the bull we rented," Mother said as I watched the tractor turn toward us at the far end of the field. "All he wants is to mount a cow. He doesn't care which one, as long as it will hold still. And when he's done with her, he'll chase another."

I watched my stepfather get down from the tractor and head our way. He climbed into the truck. "What you guys talking about?" he asked.

"Oh, you know," said Mother, "Dallas and all that and so forth and so on."

He laughed. "Yep, so forth and so on. He didn't need to buy the cow when the milk was free."

Patsy came to visit the next weekend, and we slept on the roof of our front porch because it was too hot in the house, and no breeze could stir itself up enough to bring breath to our nostrils. I told her about seeing those girls on the swings just days before Dallas eloped. I told her about the rumors that Dallas might have been pregnant, leaving out the lectures I had been given. I told her I really liked Dougie who had a car, and how I was allowed to go with him on dates for school functions or to the movies. I had to be home by 10 or half an hour after an event ended, whichever came first. If I didn't come into the house within three minutes of arriving home, Mother would switch on the porch light. I fell to sleep thinking about summer dresses, about love, about marriage and how different it was in my mind from weddings.

It's hard to say who woke up first, but late in the night, both Patsy and I sat up together looking at a fire down across the fields, about a mile or so away.

"It's the Langfeld's place," my stepfather shouted. He was already in the truck. He cranked the ignition and drove past our house, the tires spitting gravel as he went. Patsy and I watched the lights of his truck as he sped down the blacktop toward town. After we couldn't see the truck anymore, we went downstairs to be with Mother. My stepfather returned hours later and told us the Langfeld house had burned "clean to the ground." Like a lot of other people, we drove by to gawk at it the next day. We talked about the rumors that both old Mrs.

Langfeld and her granddaughter Tennessee had died in the fire and how Dallas had escaped. I wondered aloud how it felt to be spared, to be saved by love. As we stared at the still-smoldering heap of what was once a house, I pointed out to Patsy that the swings remained, untouched by the fire.

In the summer of '57, our senior year in high school, Patsy and I drove to town to Glatha's, our favorite place for root beer floats. On the way we stopped at the ruins where Mrs. Langfeld's house had been. A mound of weeds and a raised pump handle were all that was left of the old house. Even the swings were gone by now, and when I looked up, I saw that just a few feet of frayed rope hung from the tree.

We sat in the grass and recalled the rumors we had heard about Dallas's escape from being stuck at her grandma's house and how her life was saved just a few days before the big fire. I told my usual part of the story, adding embellishments as I went along.

"Tennessee wrapped the sheet tight around the bedstead. She held her breath as Dallas descended. Tennessee was wearing a printed cotton peignoir over a matching nightgown."

"What was Dallas wearing?" asked Patsy. She settled back onto the grass, hands behind her head.

"Dallas was gorgeous in a white square-necked dress with scallops at the bodice. Her skirt was gathered, accentuating her tiny waist, and she wore crinolines to make the skirt fuller. When she fell to love—and it was a great distance, Patsy—her dress billowed like a peony suddenly opening. Because her lover was so strong, he caught her and spun her around three times while they quietly laughed into each other's necks."

We still believed in love.

I dropped back onto the ground next to Patsy. We lay there for a few more minutes staring up at the whitish-blue summer sky. The story seemed to have lost some of its luster now that we were making plans for college. Patsy wanted to go to the Normal School and study to become a teacher. I was ambivalent because I felt I had options. I could be an actress; I could marry Dougie, who planned to join the Army and wanted me to live in the town next to his barracks; or, I could go to college. My mother had made all the plans for me to attend Eastern State where she said I could study theater in preparation for Hollywood. She had made all the calls to get me into school there and had even found a room for me in the new dorms the college had built.

"What is ever going to happen for us, Patsy?"

"I don't know, but I do know I'm going to college. What else is there to do?"

"Dougie wants to try to get on at Caterpillar for the summer, and he wants me to work at Glatha's. We could save money and elope. He says we'll have a summer of love and then seal it."

Patsy scrunched up her face. "What does *that* mean?"

I turned on my side away from Patsy. "He wants to go all the way."

"What?"

We lay in silence.

I couldn't tell Patsy about the date Dougie and I had when we were supposed to go to the softball game. Instead, we drove deep into the country and parked. Dougie had said we needed to talk. He told me about his dreams for our summer. We kissed, we petted, and as my curfew came closer, Dougie's hand went under my T-shirt and lay insistently across my bra. My heart had pounded against his hand. We froze.

I pulled away. "Please, stop, please. I can't be late. I'll be grounded."

"Grounded! You're too old for that." Dougie slid forcefully away, pulling himself with the steering wheel. "That's why we need to get married."

We didn't talk during the drive home. I knew he was mad at me. When he reached our lane, he stopped the car, turned to me, lifted my legs and twirled me around until I was flat against the seat and he was on top of me. He kissed me. Oh, his wonderful kisses! So soft, so urgent. His weight on me was thrilling and terrifying. I felt caught in two worlds, one of excitement and one of fear. When the bull came into my mind, when I thought of cows and free milk, the porch light came on.

He whispered, "I can't wait much longer. It's not fair. It's not right."

He lifted himself. I crawled out from under him, opened the car door and ran to my house. He called out something to me, but the sound of my shoes on our gravel drive drowned out his words. No, I couldn't tell Patsy this part. It wasn't a story of love, but I didn't know what else to call it. I had no words for it.

"We better get out of here before we get bit by chiggers." I jumped up, wiped my backside, then put out a hand to help Patsy get up.

"Do you think anyone will ever ask either of us to climb down a bed sheet?" Patsy asked as she rose.

In those final days of high school, Mother decided to turn my bedroom into a guest room. The first purchase she said she wanted was "something with a little class." She wanted a brass bed to turn her farmhouse into a country home. Mother, always looking for a bargain, had heard that some poor folks on the other side of town had one they were willing to sell.

As our truck pulled into their lane, I saw how poor these people really were, a kind of poor I had only read about at school in required books about the Great Depression. The house was big with a wraparound porch and had a Victorian look about it. Paint had peeled away from the house and several posts of the balustrade were missing.

We got out of the car; I hung back, as usual, while Mother pressed forward. A man sat on the porch step, cleaning his fingernails. As Mother approached, he stood, snapping a pocketknife closed. He wore stained bib overalls and a flannel shirt with tears at the elbows. A toothpick rested at the corner of his mouth. He and Mother said hello, and she engaged him in conversation about himself, his family and life in general. She was good at that. As the two talked, the porch filled with others members of the family. His wife, a small woman in a faded housedress made from feed sacks, held a baby in her skinny arms. Several children of various ages gathered around her, their unwashed hair strung around dirty faces.

"You come here for the bed?" He pointed to the brass head and foot rails leaning against the side of the house. Did we want them? Yes. How much were they? What would we give? And as Mother came up with an amount I can't remember, his toothpick moved back and forth between his teeth. Mother added a little extra money to "get something for the kids."

He offered to sell the mattress, too. Stained and ripped, it was folded over a chair. Mother declined the offer. As he loaded the bed into the truck, he glanced my way and said, "Who's this with ya?"

"Oh, this is my daughter. She's getting ready to go to college at Eastern. The bed is for her room."

He stopped loading the bedstead and dangled his arm over it as though it were a fence. He looked at the whole of me, wandering the surface of my body with his eyes and working that toothpick between his teeth again. He shook his head. "Shoot," he said, "she don't need to go to no school to learn what she's gonna hafta know."

Just as my eyes looked down, I heard Mother say, "That's what you think."

"That sonofabitch," my mother said as we drove down the lane. "Why in hell Dallas ever married such a man as that, I'll never know."

That was Dallas? That skinny, pinch-faced woman? And that horrible man? Was he really the one who caught her on her love-fall that summer night four years ago? Did they really spin around and laugh into each other's necks? This place, this circumstance—how could it be a testament to true love?

It was only a few years later that Patsy and I drifted apart. She had finished college, gotten married and become a teacher up near Chicago. I had taken a semester off to follow my dream to be in the movies. Mother had arranged a visit to an acting school in Hollywood for me. The halls of the school were filled with easy chairs, sofas and students lying across them reading scripts aloud with one another or by themselves. I felt self-conscious walking by them. They seemed so sophisticated, as though they knew a secret about life that was hidden from me. In one of the classes, I was mortified when the teacher asked me to read a scene with one of the boys. No one applauded when we finished. I sat down. "Would you ever consider doing that scene in the nude?" the teacher asked. When he walked me to the office, he invited me to have a drink with him that evening so he could show me stories he had written for *True Confessions*. He said he needed a Midwestern opinion. The last thing I saw as I left the school was a couple lying on the floor making out, removing each other's clothes. I knew then that I wanted to go back home to finish college.

The day I got Mother's call, I was a senior at Eastern working on my final essay for English in my dorm room. Angry feelings about this essay had been bubbling up inside me. Why had I chosen such a difficult topic? It seemed clever and imaginative when I had first announced it in class: comparing Shakespeare's Marc Antony to Salinger's Holden Caulfield. I paced my room, and ended up staring out at a broken tree, as I had so often, searching each branch for some kind of inspiration. That's when Mother's phone call interrupted me.

She called to tell me that Dallas's husband had lined Dallas and all his children against the wall of the living room during a drunken tirade and threatened to murder them with his shotgun. People were saying that Dallas had begged him to let her kill herself and the baby inside her first. He thought it a good idea, apparently, because he turned the shotgun over to her.

She blasted him out of this existence.

"All those poor kids," my mother said. "And she's been arrested."

After we hung up, I paced the room again. I thought of bed sheets hanging out of second-story windows, billowing skirts, kisses through laughing lips, fires and frayed ropes. What was true? What was a lie? I imagined the house and entered it: a stark room, a pregnant woman, children lined against a wall, a shotgun, blood spattered across peeling wallpaper. What is love? How does it lead to this room?

I looked down at my typewriter with the empty sheet of paper rolled into it. My pile of books and random notes lay carelessly across the desk. I typed furiously for several pages. I read what I had written and realized I was writing about love, about Holden Caulfield's love of innocence, about Marc Antony's love for justice. Okay, it needed work, but I had begun, and I was eager to return to a love with few regrets, a safe love, a love that would not fail me.

I stacked my papers neatly on my desk. Old images I shared with my best friend from high school came to me: colors, cummerbunds, tiered cakes, break-up songs. *And now*, I thought, *I have to call Patsy.* She had to know about this cruel love. Together we would separate truth from fantasy, try to understand love, its follies, its foibles and, perhaps, its healing. Then I would talk to her about school and my deepening love for learning. I would remind her of the day Mother and I bought the bed and how that man told me school would never teach me what I had to know—how that moment led to this one.

Judy Jones *was once an adventurer, traveling in disguise as a college professor in places such as California, New Hampshire, Illinois, Macau and Beijing, China. Now, as she lives and breathes the troubled air of Mishawaka, Indiana, her travels are inward and follow a path from various inner realms to a page. For a while, she told the truth in poems and prose, but has begun to realize how much fun writing can be when she lies. Politicians do it all the time; so, why not? Fiction beckons her.*

YOUNG, *YOUNG* LADIES

Will Link

PEOPLE TELL YOU NOT TO LOOK FOR LOVE. They say, "When you stop looking for it, *it* will find *you*." These people… are assholes.

Most of these assholes are also in long-standing relationships. What they don't remember is that dating is hard. That's why I have always taken the opposite approach to love. Don't wait for the time to be right. Don't wait until you have money to take her out with or a job you're actually happy with or until you've moved out of your parents' basement in Lake Ronkonkoma, Long Island. These things will never happen anyway. So I say you should be willing to completely and utterly give your heart over to literally *anyone* you meet at *any* given time.

Now, I know what you're thinking: This sounds like the horrible advice of a sad, desperate man. But think about it. How many times have you met a member of the opposite sex and didn't ask him out because he had just gotten out of a relationship? Or you felt you just didn't have the time in your own life? Or she happened to be dating your brother? You felt the timing just wasn't right. And now think about how much, as you lie dying alone on your death bed, you'll regret that decision.

Of course the downside to my approach of taking a chance on everyone is that *everyone* is fucking insane. But don't wait...the time will never be just right for perfect mental health.

Over the years, many well-intentioned friends have tried to deter me from the women I've dated. For me, there was the stereotypical flaky L.A. actress. The controlling Persian who wouldn't let me hold her hand in Westwood out of fear the other Persians might see. The girl into polyamory who, wouldn't you know, *couldn't* commit. The girl who claimed she was incapable of love who proceeded to never love me. And of course the alcoholic who tried to urinate in my bathroom sink. I was warned ahead of time not to pursue any of these lovely ladies. I did anyway because I'm a firm believer in "you meet who you meet," warnings of friends be damned. In recent years, however, I've heard one warning over and over. A warning I was determined to ignore again and again: "Don't date girls who just turned 21!"

I've never been the man who went after women more than a decade younger than I was. But lately those are the women I've had the best luck with. Probably because they're too young to realize I'm basically a failure. A girl my own age realizes my job is dead-end and my apartment is in the valley. A girl just out of college sees me having a job and my own apartment as a success. So when I meet a young, *young* lady, it's hard for me to turn her away.

I was at my local karaoke bar one night when, for some unforeseen reason, a trio of beautiful women sat down with my friends and me. We all sang and drank the night away. The cutest of the three was Casey. Blonde, thin, large breasts, nerdy glasses and an ever-so-slight Australian accent. As the evening wore on, she and I started to talk more and more. It seemed like we were hitting it off as well as two people can over a deafening karaoke rendition of "Livin' on a Prayer." At one point in the night, someone sang Lisa Loeb's "Stay." Since everyone at the table remembered when this song was the biggest thing on radio, we all sang along. Everyone, that is, except Casey.

"Why aren't you singing along?" I asked. "Don't you know it?"

"When did it come out?"

"1994?"

She thought for a moment. "Oh…I was only two years old."

I wondered if I should check her ID to see if legally she should even be in a bar, but then I remembered the bouncer had done this for me. Was she at least mature for her age, you ask? *Absolutely not*. Her life seemed directionless, more preoccupied with drinking than doing anything else.

Some would say her being 21 was a red flag I chose to ignore. But the bigger red flag came next.

"I'm surprised I'm so attracted to you," she told me.

"Why's that?"

"Because I don't really like Jews."

I should have walked away from the situation right then and there. How could I date an anti-Semite? That said, despite my appearance and neurotic behavior, I'm actually *not* Jewish. Plus, this may have been the most conventionally beautiful woman who ever wanted me. I tried to justify her hate. She's immature and doesn't choose her words carefully. She's Australian. Maybe it's an Australian thing to hate the Jews. So rather than call her out on the bigotry, I simply said, "Well, it's a good thing I'm not Jewish." She looked relieved.

We went on a date to the zoo. There I learned more and more about her life. For example, her mother and father had recently divorced, yet her father still lived in their garage where he made money by raising poisonous snakes. Also, Casey worked part-time teaching art to children. She liked her job but seemed to have an issue with her bosses. I asked what was wrong.

"They're such Jews!" she shouted.

My mouth dropped wide open and my head spun around. "Don't worry," she said trying to calm me. "There are none around."

Lovingly I grabbed her hand and explained to her that you can't just yell "Jew" like that. My friends had warned me that dating a 21-year-old would involve a lot of teaching, and clearly Casey wasn't the brightest bulb. They also warned me that all she'd want to do was party. They were right. Every night she wanted to drink and be out until 4 a.m. I wanted to watch a movie and be in bed by 10. At the end of the day, it wasn't anti-Semitism that made me end it—it was anti-sleepism. I was literally just too exhausted by the prospect of seeing her. Plus, being with Casey made me feel old. Much older than my 34 years.

And that's also one of the reasons I'm willing to take a chance on dating a bigoted lunatic. When I was younger, I did wait. I waited too long to move to Los Angeles. I waited too long to start getting up on a stage to tell stories. And too many times, I waited too damn long to ask for a girl's phone number. Now that I'm in my mid-30s, I wait no more. I'm up for anything.

So, obviously, that means I didn't learn my lesson.

A few months later, I was at the same karaoke bar when I met Alysha. She was actually there on a date, but it was clear to everyone in the bar, except her clueless beau, that she only had eyes for me. We slipped each other our numbers under the table. It wasn't until later that I discovered she, too, had just reached the drinking age.

Not all 21-year-olds are alike. Unlike Casey, Alysha wasn't dumb and just wanting to party. Alysha was just *green*. She had high-minded dreams. The kind of dreams we older folks gave up on long ago. Hers was to be the next Oprah. I'd listen to her talk about her goals and I'd smile, knowing what the realities of life would actually dish out. I wanted to give her a shot, though. My ageist friends couldn't be right about *all* 21-year-olds!

The big problem came when we tried to have sex. We couldn't. I mean we physically couldn't! My penis could not penetrate her vagina. You see, Alysha was a virgin with a lot of sexual anxieties that cause her to tighten up. She'd even gone to a doctor about this and was given apparatuses to use on herself to…open up more.

Was this a byproduct of her youth and thus another strike against 21-year-olds? Had she not had time in life to experiment sexually, or was this a physical issue she would have to deal with at any age? Although not opposed to it, I had never taken someone's virginity. My first girlfriend had a reputation. She had had sex with quite a few boys before me because she liked sex. This girl was a beautiful, thoughtful person, and never for a second did her history deter me from wanting to be in a relationship with her. There's no such thing as a "slut." I assumed my virginal 16-year-old self would enjoy sex just as much as she. I did. Very early on in our relationship, she gave me my first blow job, and to this day it remains the most seminal moment in my sexual life.

Much more so than losing my virginity. I was thankful to learn everything about sex from an experienced woman my own age.

Nearly 20 years later, I found myself in the teacher role, and I wasn't sure if I should answer the call or not. Because of Alysha's greenness, I realized this wasn't a woman I could be with long-term anyway. If anything, this would just be a sexual fling—*apparently* without the sex. We tried a few times unsuccessfully, and I got more and more nervous. Did I even *want* to take her virginity? I felt like I'd just be using her. So I ended things before they went too far. Alysha did not take it well.

"I don't see a future between us," I said. "I don't want to be an asshole and just take your virginity."

"You're an asshole because you *didn't* take my virginity! You're the closest I ever came to having sex!" she screamed at me. "*Now I'll never have sex!*"

"Did you really want me to take your virginity and then just break up with you?"

"Yes!?! And you'll regret this."

I didn't have to regret it for long. A month later she texted me that she was moving to Pittsburgh. We got together the next day, and I took her virginity on my IKEA sofa. She speculated that I was able to break through the once-impenetrable barrier because she was simultaneously comfortable physically with me and was no longer nervous and invested in the idea of a relationship. In the weeks before she moved, we had a lot of sex. I did become the teacher. She would show up at my place wanting to try a new position each time. Afterward, she was always sure to tell me how awful a person I was, just like any mature 21-year-old would.

An anti-Semite and a virgin. So far, 21-year-olds weren't working out. But I still couldn't listen to my friends. You meet who you meet, and it's not like they were introducing me to anyone my own age. One night at the very same bar (which clearly must cater to a younger crowd), I met a girl who was twenty…*two*. We went out on a few dates, and the fact that she was over a decade younger was apparent. She seemed nervous when it came to dating. She didn't get references I made to films from the '80s and '90s. She mostly talked about cartoons. Sure, some of this was because she was shy and worked as an animator. But it also spoke to an inexperience that comes with being in your early 20s. Maybe they can't help it, just like I can't help being bitter and terrified of dying alone in my mid-30s.

Despite these incidents (and the failed relationships with every other woman I've ever been involved with), I still stick with my philosophy. I'll give anyone a chance, because dating is hard and you never know who that perfect person is going to be. So if you want my heart, just let me know. It's yours.

On second thought…maybe let me check some ID first.

**Will Link** has always been a storyteller. Born on Long Island, reluctantly he moved west to Los Angeles, pursuing a career in screenwriting. He took to L.A. faster than any self-respecting New Yorker should and, 10 years later, still calls it home. Since then he's worked as a film critic and on-air host for Afterbuzz TV. There, he also discovered the world of personal comedic essay writing and has performed pieces in shows across the country. He finds this medium successfully combines his love of writing and hearing the sound of his own voice. Listen to him weekly, breaking down all things pop culture on his mildly popular comedy podcast Will Sean Podcast? which you can find on iTunes. Follow him on Twitter @TheRealWillLink.

WELCOME BACK, RICHARD, TO THE CROWN AND ANCHOR

Deborah Ross

Hey, you remember my name.

Of course I remember your name. We went to high school together. We were best friends for nine years, married for five. Even after the divorce, we saw each other for drinks at least once a year, in February, the month of both our birthdays. You even agreed to meet me at Gordon Biersch and drink weird German lager when you really would have been happier at Hooters where you could get a Bud and watch the game, because you knew the game and the noise and probably even the hooters themselves would give me a post-feminist headache. How are you?

I'd like a double cheeseburger.

Sure you would. Coming right up. I just have to remember that James, with the striped shirt, who came in before you, wants a cola and a burrito, and Linda, with the earpiece, has just come in and asked for water, and Thompson, one of the four black guys, ordered a ham sandwich a while ago and it hasn't come yet. If I get the orders wrong, I lose points, and then I have to play the game all over again. That's how these Lumosity computer games work. If you don't end up within your top-five previous scores, your overall quotient goes down for the day, and then the graph they show you at the end is a straight line down—very depressing. It sort of defeats the whole purpose of Lumosity, which they say in the commercials is supposed to be a fun way to ward off senility—not a chronicle of your mental deterioration.

The weird thing is that three of the cartoon characters who come in the restaurant look like people I know in real life who have the same names. There's Gary who looks like my nephew, and Mark who looks like my second husband. And then there's my favorite—you, Richard. The sad thing is when I start the game, I never know if you'll come back. Just my luck: usually it's Mark. Sometimes you don't show up for weeks. Sometimes this game doesn't come up at all, and by the time it does, I've forgotten which black guy is Thompson and which Asian woman is Kimberly. But I never forget you, Richard, with your yellow polo shirt that's a little too tight around the stomach, and the face that, even though it's just a cartoon, really makes me feel as if you're looking at me again through its eyes. Especially if I talk to you out loud.

May I please have some coffee?

Of course, Richard, I'm on it. But just wait a minute, will you, because the orders are up now and I have to remember who wanted chai and who wanted just regular tea. Okay, here's your coffee and cheeseburger. But please don't eat it right away, because if we get the customers' names right when they come in, they don't ask us for the checks before they leave, they just say "Bye" or "See you later," and I really need to talk to you before you go. I need your advice.

Remember when we were 21, and your mom had remarried a couple years before and moved into a house right across the street from the one I grew up in, though we didn't live there anymore, but I had actually been in your house years before because I was friends with the girl who used to live there? Who would have guessed when I was 10 and went there for a sleepover that someday I would be sneaking into bed with you in that same room, sneaking not because your mom ever invaded your space or asked any questions, but because I was supposed to be your best friend's girlfriend? Remember how you used to party back then? You'd come home so drunk every night that you would make yourself toast and then fall asleep with your head on the kitchen table, and a couple hours later Tony would come down for breakfast before going to work and find you there. And he never said a word about it, because your mom made it so clear when she married him that you were part of the deal, period.

See you later.

Oh, Richard, don't go yet. Shit.

Hello again, Richard. I'm so glad to see you, I thought you'd never come back.

Hi, how are you?

Well, not so good, really. You see, here's the thing. This is what I've been wanting to ask you about. It's my son. Really, Richard, so many times I wished he was your son, though I realize if we'd ever had kids they would have been different people anyway. No use thinking about that. The thing is, he's moved out. Actually, I sort of made him leave. This is something your mom would never do, right? No matter what, right? And that's what I always thought I would be like when I had kids.

But you see, I've been seeing different therapists at Kaiser for my depression. And mainly it's because of him that I'm depressed. You know he's always had all kinds of problems, right, ADHD and supposedly Asperger's, and he goes to Kaiser, too, for depression from having these things, or from being labeled as having them. I'm not really sure if he thinks they're real or not. You remember last time we were at Gordon Biersch around our birthdays, what I told you about his Facebook page? How my sister told me my niece told her that he had posted drawings he made in his own blood? Well, so I knew he was in trouble. And I knew he was experimenting with substances, like we did. Even when he was still in high school, I would find empty bottles of Formula 44 or Nyquil or even vodka that I guess he shoplifted from Foodland. And that one time I found a foil package with brownie crumbs on it hidden in the trunk, I took away his car keys. I know, weed isn't a big deal, but you know he really wasn't safe to drive. He almost totaled his grandma's car after she said he stole some of his grandpa's pain pills, and he's had accidents with my car, too, when he looked stoned though he said he wasn't. But I still didn't think it was that serious as long as he didn't drive. And in a way, I was kind of happy he didn't have a job or anything because if he didn't have any money, he would have to stay home where I could sort of keep an eye on him.

I'd like a hamburger.

Sure, that's right, hamburger for you, BLT sandwich and chocolate milk for Patricia, the blonde who sticks her chest out, and apple juice for Matt, the guy who keeps his hand in front of his mouth for some reason.

But so, Richard, anyways, then I started finding really scary things in his room, little cotton balls, a lighter and a spoon, these tiny Ziploc bags with what looked like white powder inside. And pieces of plastic that looked like they could come off a disposable syringe. We never did anything like that back in the day. I hardly even knew anybody who did. But what if you had? What do you think your mom would have done? I bet she would just have cried and left you notes asking where she went wrong, and you would have felt really bad for a few days and maybe even stayed in and played cards with her and Tony, or maybe not, but you still would have felt bad and thought about maybe not drinking so much. Well, I cried, too, but I don't think he even noticed. And everyone at Kaiser, my therapist, the doctor who writes my prescriptions and the two therapists who run my group, even the people *in* the group—really old hands at the therapy business because they're mainly addicts themselves—they all said I have to set boundaries. I have to say, "You can't live in my house and do drugs." If I don't, I'm enabling him to keep doing them, and it means I'm co-dependent and actually somehow want him to hurt himself because of my own sickness. Also, if I don't set boundaries, I'm allowing him to disrespect me, which will be bad for my self-esteem. Well, screw my self-esteem. Frankly, I always knew that I would feel worse than anything if he was gone and I didn't know where he was. But if I was really hurting him by not saying this, I really couldn't stand it. So I set the boundary, and of course he stepped right over it like he's been doing since he was three and his sister was born, and of course now he's gone and I feel like shit.

So what do you think, Richard? Did I do the right thing?

Please bring me coffee.

OK, I get it. You don't want to give your opinion because you think I need to figure this out for myself. That's how you always were—I would talk and talk and talk, and you would hardly say anything, and I could imagine there was all this benevolent wisdom behind your silence, or I could imagine your ears just needed a rest and shut down, there was no way to tell. But lots of times, it worked anyway because somehow I would come up with something on my own. Or you would finally say something out loud—either "just act normal," if I was driving stoned and a cop was behind us, or "fuck 'em if they can't take a joke," if I thought someone was mad at me. Well, neither of those sayings seems to apply to the situation of a son out there somewhere, God knows where, over a week now, with his phone going straight to message, and the police, for various reasons, out of the question. Is there something you're not saying but thinking I should do? Or are you just thinking you wish you could smoke in here, and you'd rather have a beer than a coffee, and it's messed up that they call this place something that sounds like a bar and then only serve sandwiches and non-alcoholic drinks, and maybe it's about time to head out to the Red Robin or the Dinghy or some other joint we used to hang out in that went out of business a long time ago but that maybe is still open in that cyberspace where you are now?

Then again, if you had quit smoking and drunk less beer, or if your mom had somehow put her foot down or set boundaries or something, maybe your lungs and liver would have lasted more than 59 years, and I wouldn't have to talk to this silly cartoon Richard with the dumb yellow polo shirt. It's worse than the slides at your funeral. I mean, it was so nice at first to see the random sequence with your high-school self at your mom's wedding, and then your grown-up self with Pua and her kids and grandkids and even the one great-grandkid, doing stuff you and I were always too burned out to do, even dancing—of all things—at some club in Vegas. She was such a good wife for you, always around and talking but mostly into her phone to her sisters and nieces and nephews, so you could listen but didn't have to answer. You even started drinking less because she didn't like it—something I was always too scared to ask you to do for me. I just taught myself how to keep up with you, till finally I couldn't. But most of the funeral slides were of you kicking back in your recliner with a cat curled up in your lap and a Bud in a styrofoam holder on one side and a pack of Kools and an ashtray on the other, watching the game, with your hair different lengths and going back and forth from brown to gray. And then after 15 minutes or so, the same slides would start to come up again in a different order, and I realized, that's all there is, there isn't any more, forever.

Until you turned up a few weeks ago, here on the computer screen in my living room.

See you later.

God, Richard, I really hope so. I remember the last thing you actually said out loud to me. When I came to see you in the hospital, you and Pua were planning a farewell picnic for when you got out, and I said don't forget to invite me, and even though I know I drove you up a wall all those years, you said, "I could never forget you." And it just sort of hung there in the air like smoke: how long is never?

Well, now I imagine what you meant was that you should never let go of people you love, no matter what they do. So next time you come to the Crown and Anchor, of course I'll remember your name. And I'll try really hard, when you do, to get your order right.

**Deborah Ross**, *a not-yet-retired English professor at Hawaii Pacific University, moved to Hawaii from upstate New York in 1980, causing severe culture shock from which she has yet to recover. She now lives in a family-oriented suburban neighborhood in Waipahu — far from ideal for a single woman with grown children, though good for her dog, Genji — and is trying to figure out where the two of them should go for the next phase of her life. Meanwhile, while still tossing out the occasional academic paper, she tries to write amusingly about addiction, anxiety, Asperger's — basically the whole DSM — believing that all these conditions, along with the rapidly increasing bereavements that come with aging, must have a lighter side. See her web page at http://www.hpu.edu/CHSS/English/Faculty/EFRoss.html.*

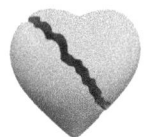

CONFESSIONS OF MY DYING FATHER

Stevie Leigh

ON EASTER SUNDAY, MY FATHER TOLD ME—his lesbian daughter, his youngest child—his deepest, darkest secret. Did he tell me because he was dying? Did he tell me simply because I was the one who had asked him to take a walk? Did he tell me because he knew that I knew what it was like to live in secret, to avoid the truth, to lie to myself every day?

We were on the sidewalk outside my sister's house. The sun was warm. The breeze was slight but the air was cold. His lips were red. Not bright red, but a red I never recognized before, almost maroon. He wore a red cardigan, so maybe that had something to do with it. His lips were like mine: the top one thin, the bottom one plump. I don't remember ever before being that close to his face for that amount of time. I knew, though, that if I kept my face close enough to his face and stayed close enough, long enough, he would tell me what he was convinced would break him. His lips were also moist, not dry. This surprised me because one of his medications caused dry mouth. As he brought his cigarette to his mouth, he held it there on the top of his bottom lip, rolled it back and forth between his thumb and index finger, and then took a long drag before he would talk.

My father confessed that he had lied about having bareback sex with female prostitutes while still sexually engaged with my mother. My father had never used protection with my mother throughout their 49-year marriage and their one-year engagement. Until that Easter Sunday, my father never admitted that he was fucking professional sex workers without a condom in the AIDS era and beyond.

"I'm sorry," he said. I'm sure this is pretty common between the dying and the ones they love. "I'm sorry." Not "I love you." But "I'm sorry." Not "I'll miss you." But "I'm sorry."

"You are forgiven," I said back to him. Not "Go to hell." "You are forgiven." Not "How could you?" "You are forgiven. You are forgiven."

My father paused, or stopped talking altogether. I knew he wasn't with me anymore. He was back there in those places, in those moments, with those people.

Now, inside again, in the aftermath of his confession, my father paced around the room, not wanting to sit still.

He was weak but anxious. So much of his muscle mass had dissolved since the New Year. He needed walls or furniture to help stabilize him, to stand up and to sit down. He had lost a lot of weight fast. Estrogen pumped through his body now, suppressing his male hormones. "Gotta get the PSA level down," he would say. Prostate-specific antigen. Side effects of estrogen include: (1) erection problems, (2) hot flushes and sweating, (3) weakness and fatigue, (4) breast tenderness, (5) tumor flare pain and (6) mood swings and depression. His testosterone was depleted and estrogen was overtaking his body. His nature shifted hard, and it shifted fast. He wanted to talk. He wanted to talk about how he felt. He wanted to talk about his feelings. He wanted to talk about his feelings? That's not my dad. He would cry at the slightest thing or for no reason at all. My dad didn't cry. He didn't talk about his feelings. How could estrogen turn my dad into a man who wanted to express his feelings? Hormones tell our brains what do to. Death tells our consciences what to do.

Estrogen and confronting his own death had made my father the man I wanted to know. They made me want to trust him with my emotions. He was funny. He was open. He was sad. He was sorry. To know this man, I needed to hear his confession. With his confession, he gave me a profound gift. He shared his soul with me.

I'm sure it's pretty common for adult children to eventually discover their parents' lies. I completely understand why my father hid his behavior. He paid for sex for more than 20 years, he told me. He said it was over the last 20 years of his marriage. He paid for sex as often as he could, traveling back and forth from Ohio to Michigan for as long as he could. Once his prostate became diseased, he could no longer climax. I never asked him, but I wondered how much money he spent on sex for his 20-plus-year indulgence. How many women he fucked who were being trafficked. He called it an addiction. He thought it was wrong. He wanted to stop. He knew he risked his reputation. He knew he risked my mom's reputation. He knew he risked his marriage. He couldn't stop. He said he couldn't stop. He said he knew plenty of other guys who did it, too.

My father had been a barber for more than 40 years. A barbershop is filled with "guy's guys." It's a place where men of different ages, who like to be in each other's company, smoke pipes, cigarettes and cigars while discussing politics, sports, woodworking and where to buy sex. A barbershop smells like nicotine, hair tonic and men. Lusting for women is pretty common in barbershops. The barbershop is a men's club where women enter only to escort their men. Mothers bring their sons, wives bring their husbands and daughters bring their fathers. But the women don't stay long. Often they wait in the car or go on errands. Across from his barber's chair, my dad had mounted a magazine rack. An aesthetic-looking object, made from hardwood, mid-century modern style, made with thin, sleek, elegant lines. The magazine rack contained *Popular Mechanics, Car and Driver, This Old House, Men's*

Health and, my personal favorite, *Sports Illustrated*. These magazines were for public display, to be read in a public setting. In the back room, there was an extensive collection of *Playboy* magazines. He told me he read *Playboy* for the articles. He stocked a few *Maxims* but not any *Penthouse*. He said *Penthouse* was "too raunchy."

I'm not exactly sure how it worked because I didn't really witness the culture firsthand. The men behaved differently when I, as a little girl and later as a young woman, was in the shop. Or at least I thought so. But I imagine men of different ages would go to the bathroom and then step into the back room for a bit of "reading." Or perhaps they would first fetch the magazine so they had some "reading" while they shat. Every now and again, my brother would sneak some magazines back to his bedroom, unaware that I was a notorious snoop. I found my sister's diaphragm in her dresser drawer one night. I showed it to my mom and said, "What is this?" She asked me where I found it. "Under the bathroom sink," I said. "Put it back," she said. Once I realized what it was, I couldn't figure out how it worked. I found the *Playboy*s in my brother's closet buried under stuffed animals and some smelly, sticky clothes. I found an 8mm stag film. I tried to look at it by holding the film up to the light, resting it against the window like a light table, but the frames were too small to see anything but butts and what I thought were balls.

My brother caught me one day reading the magazine. He called me a dyke. "I'm reading an article about Christopher Reeve in the *Superman* movie," I said. I really was. He didn't believe me. Sometimes, though, I'd look at naked men because seeing a man's penis gave me something to talk about with my best friend, Lisa. There weren't many naked men in *Playboy*. The stories were about men and told from men's points of view, but there were rarely any pictures of naked men. The pictures of the women embarrassed me. Their facial expressions confused me. Their hair was super-puffy. I always wondered how much hairspray they used, and then I wondered if they used Aqua Net or White Rain. Hairspray made me wheeze and sneeze. The women wore a lot of makeup, too. When I kissed my mom and she had makeup on, it tasted gross, like paste with perfume in it. These women weren't erotic to me, but at that age, nothing was. In my teens, I was the classic asexual tomboy on the outside, the P-type body who wanted to be a boy but who lacked testosterone.

My father was diagnosed with stage IV prostate cancer in January 2009 and was dead nine months later. Cancer ate up his lungs and bones. Radiation couldn't burn away all those cells. Chemotherapy was not an option. He was a dead man who denied the truth at first and shifted the responsibility to the doctors whom he would never consult. "They didn't catch it soon enough," he said. He hid his body so he wouldn't get caught fucking prostitutes. He hid his sickness so he wouldn't get caught fucking prostitutes. He shrank when they removed the fluid from his body. He shrank to half his size. His bloated gut vanished. His fat face narrowed and now looked drawn and drained. His eyes sunk deep into his skull. He had asked me to stop making him look so fat in the pictures that I had taken of him before his diagnosis. I only know of one picture that was taken of him after he was diagnosed. He's sitting in a red wheelchair, wearing a bright purple sweatshirt with a canary-yellow blanket over his legs watching a high school football game.

After his confession, my mother told me that it "would take forever" to get my dad off. Yet another side effect that they both chose to ignore, but maybe it was just my mother. Maybe it didn't take forever in the massage parlor where he met the prostitutes. My father rarely saw a doctor in a doctor's office. I asked him if he avoided getting checkups because he thought he'd get caught. He said yes and then he started to cry. When he needed medications, the doctors that he barbered would give him prescriptions. In his 50s, he got poison ivy on his dick. The skin lacerations wouldn't heal, so he asked one of his doctor customers for medicine. After he requested a third refill, the doctor insisted on an office exam. He didn't have an STD as he feared, but he did have type 2 diabetes.

Once his blood filled with the estrogen that killed the testosterone that was killing him, my father became paranoid. He hallucinated. He said the chicken on the placemat wanted him to die. He told me one time that I wanted him to die. He told me that he had given Mom AIDS. He said that he had AIDS, and he pointed to a clogged pore on his eyelid. It was the size of a pinhead. I asked him if he had ever seen an AIDS patient with skin lesions. He said, "No." Never in my life did I imagine that I would be showing my father pictures of AIDS patients with skin lesions because he thought he had gotten AIDS from having unprotected sex with female prostitutes and that he had given AIDS to my mother. But there I was, showing my father pictures of AIDS patients with skin lesions because he thought he had gotten AIDS from having unprotected sex with female prostitutes and that he had given AIDS to my mother. There I was, thinking that they should put pictures of AIDS patients with skin lesions in *Playboy* magazine.

I always thought that my parents, in the beginning of their relationship, were best friends. I fell in love with the story of how they met. My mom and dad met at a county fair. The story goes that my dad, looking like Kevin Costner in *A Perfect World,* was a sexy young man with confidence and a cocky smile, and he knew right away that he wanted my mom. The story says that he refused her admittance to the fair until she went across the street to get him cigarettes. He gave her the money. He needed to smoke but couldn't leave his post. He took a Camel (no filter) out of the package, rolled the package up in the sleeve of his white T-shirt and asked her for a light. They dated for a year. My mom broke it off once or twice, and the story goes that she broke his heart. He'd go over to her mother's house and cry. He went to visit my mom after her appendectomy when she was 17, and she told him to leave. My mom dated a guy or two after the breakup, but ultimately they got back together. They married at 18 years of age. The story goes they got married in August, went on a Niagara Falls honeymoon and had their first child, my sister, nine months later. Then came their son and, soon after his birth, they bought their first and only house. Then they had me, their youngest daughter. The story goes that the wife outlived the husband, who died nearly 50 years after they married, and that everything she thought her marriage had been, she now thought was a lie.

My father saw ghosts. He asked me who was playing golf out on the lawn. He made my hair stand up on the back of my neck a few times. He was never afraid of what he saw, though. He asked me who was standing by the bed wearing a ball hat. In his room, we played Zen music at nighttime. We played Dean Martin and other crooners during the day. He had sundowner's syndrome toward the end, before he went on morphine. He wouldn't sleep; he'd want to be up moving around. A loud thud in the middle of the night woke me once. He fell off the toilet and hit his head. I didn't sleep upstairs again until the night he died.

He wanted to talk then. He tried to tell me things he never could before. I listened, and I would ask questions when I wanted to know more. He asked, "Was I too hard on you?" I told him he was. "Do you trust me?" he said. "Not with my emotions," I said. He talked about his childhood. I asked him if he looked at pornography as a child, as a young man. He said, "No, I was afraid Grandma would catch me." I asked him if he was ever molested. He said, "No." I searched for evidence that proved he became a sex addict at a young age and that his behavior didn't develop as an adult, but I couldn't find that evidence. He said he was a sex addict. He said he tried, but he couldn't stop.

Sex addict? Did he have a medical problem, or did he have a social problem? I found self-help groups like Sex Addicts Anonymous, Sexual Compulsives Anonymous and Sexaholics Anonymous. I read books on the subject. Sex addicts had constructed a grassroots movement, like Alcoholics Anonymous, and had declared disease status for their disorder before the AMA proclaimed their disorder to be a disease. Sex addiction has been *medicalized*. It's legit. My father combined the right (and wrong) amounts of pleasure and pain to produce his addiction. Standing there in the warm afternoon light, with the bright blue sky above us, his red sweater absorbing the cigarette smoke coming out of his nose and mouth, he was reliving the pleasure of fucking prostitutes as he spoke to me. As he rolled his cigarette across his moist red lips, he was there fucking them again, bareback.

My father was an addict. He was immune to any moral wrongdoing. But he was never medically diagnosed as a sex addict, and he never went to a sex addicts support group. He fucked as many prostitutes as he could for as long as he could. In the end, I'm left with wondering what he was. Was he an addict or an asshole? In the end, he was a barber, my mother's husband, my father and a liar. I'm thankful every day that he shared his lies with me. I may never be able to understand why he did what he did, but he told me the truth, the awful truth about who he was and what he did. He shared his life with me. He let me in.

Stevie Leigh *lives in Ohio—"the heart of it all"—surrounded by farmland, buffer zones and refuge zones. Other than being inundated with pesticides, herbicides and neonicotinoids, her homeland is quite peaceful and picturesque. She loves her wife, her son, her dogs, marijuana and dogs who love marijuana.*

DISSOLVE

Amanda Roskos

"What's this word mean, Mom?" I shoved the book in my mom's face while she was at the dining room table. She was studying for an exam and had a mug filled with carrots, as she liked to eat while studying and didn't want to consume a bag of M&Ms or Twizzlers like she had the week before.

Without even looking up from the workbook, she said, "You know where the dictionary is."

"You didn't even look at the word," I said and shook my book at her. "Just look."

"I don't need to."

"You don't need to 'cause you don't know."

"Yes. That's it." My mom was brilliant at playing Boggle, Scrabble and pretty much all word games, and when she won, if she were a footballer, she would have done a victory dance worthy of Billy "White Shoes"

Johnson's "funky chicken." When she lost, which was rare, you could tell it rankled. It was in the downturn of her mouth, the tightness in her lips and a flash of irritation in the eyes. Just a flash.

"Can you at least tell me how to pronounce it?"

Mom looked up and removed my index finger and said, "*Dissolve.*"

"Could you use it in a sentence?"

"Dictionary." She pointed yonder.

"Fine," I huffed and hefted the dictionary from its repository under a low table. There were a few cacti lounging on the top part. The bottom shelf held the giant tome: The Random House Dictionary of the English Language, unabridged version, circa 1966. This was purchased with my mom's first paycheck from the elementary school where she worked part-time as a kindergarten teacher. It had these beautiful grooves for each letter of the alphabet. Those were my favorite things. I used to think little alphabet fairies lived there, and when I would press on them, they would tickle the fleshy pads of my fingers or thumbs.

> ***Dissolve**: a. to cause to disperse or disappear: destroy; b. to separate into component parts: disintegrate; c. to bring to an end: terminate (dissolve parliament).*

I thought *perfect, that's what has happened to us. Our family has dissolved.* But I didn't use that in a sentence.

"Sugar *dissolves* in hot liquids," I said as proof that I understood.

"Good," she said and went on studying and chomping carrots.

I don't remember the day my dad left, only the ripples of his leaving. I went back to sleeping on the stone entryway, which always upset my mom. When I was first brought home from the orphanage, I used to sleep there or on the floor by my bed, most likely because I was used to sleeping on the ground in Korea. Besides being cool in the summer and slightly irregular in texture, color and pattern, there was something enormously satisfying about the sound of things on the entryway stone. I used to press my ear there and hear the beat of the house. It was a thud, an echo, a rumbling of movement deep in the center of the family. This spot was also where my dad and I had held many tap-dance extravaganzas Sunday mornings waiting for Mom to get ready for church. Mom would come down the stairs and yell at us, "Stop that! You're scratching up the entryway!" Dad's response was always some loose interpretation of a Russian or Double Wings sequence, with a wink to me. Now, I traced the many scratches that his brown leather ankle boots and my black patent Mary Janes had created while doing our favorite vaudeville act. Dad would say, "Gene Kelly's got nothing on us," as he did a riff, a slurp and a paradiddle. My older brother, Theo, could be heard to say, "More like Gene Kelly would throw up in his towel."

Over time, the ripples grew wider. The kids in the neighborhood whispered behind our backs, and the teachers' oh-so-kind tones of voice when speaking to me indicated that a tragedy had occurred in my family. These kindnesses were annoying to me as they interfered with fabricating an attitude that nothing had changed, that everything was hunky-dory, as my grandma would say. They especially got in the way when I would tell elaborate tales of how my father had gone to New York City to cure some random childhood disease, like lymphoma, and that *that* was the reason he was gone all the time. Inevitably the kids found out and some called me out on the lie but most just began to avoid me. Then our family dog, Bandit, got run over by a car. Bandit was a black and white Border collie mix with a black mask around his eyes, hence the name. He was my brother's first dog and my natural nemesis; having been in the family before me, he was convinced I didn't belong. Also, he couldn't resist chasing cars. It was his favorite hobby, besides bird-finding, fetching and tagging along after Theo.

After Dad moved three hours away with his 20-year-old secretary and set up house, an old Victorian with a rocking chair on the porch, Mom took over the responsibilities of our house and garden, the station wagon and us. Truth be told, everything became a little neglected.

The ivy usurped the zucchini and eggplant garden. It climbed up the side of the house, all the way to the roof, and wormed its way into the gutter drains, which Mom eventually had to hire someone to clean out. Something always seemed to be breaking or about to break. Since Mom's only job experience—as a part-time kindergarten teacher—hadn't garnered much financial security, she took an entry-level position and went to night school. I don't remember how many years Mom worked at a manufacturing company. I think it was until she got her second degree and started to work for some firm.

My mom made it her mission to make sure nothing else changed in our lives. She refused my grandparents' suggestion to come live with them in Florida so they could help her, and she ignored her sister's urging to move to Ohio to be closer to family. So we lived in that split-level two-story house that my parents had picked out together with a large backyard and two side yards (one for my mom's tomatoes and zucchini, and the other for my brother's lookout tree, where he would pelt unsuspecting neighborhood kids and his pesky little sister—me!—with acorns from his slingshot) until after I went off to college.

We were down one dad and one dog. But the worst thing that happened were the words we never spoke. Breakfast and dinner became a time when we pretended that we were okay. I hid behind cereal boxes, trying to read the smallest print, or I snuck library books on my lap while Theo let his long bangs cover his eyes. He would eat fast so he could get back to his bedroom, his music and whatever he did to pass the excruciating hours before the next day. Mom never sat very long, usually eating while getting something from the drawers, or turning off the stove, or putting something in the sink. Most of this was done while asking us how our day went or telling us something about *her* day. She always acted like the boring things that happened at work were interesting. I would take hours to eat dinner, chewing every bite 22 times like the heroine from a long-forgotten book.

Dad's absence took up residence at dinner—the empty chair that never got filled no matter how often I played musical chairs—and even more so during the time before I fell asleep. There were monsters lurking under my bed and in my closet. I never understood why bedrooms had so many places for scary things to hide in…dolls on bookshelves turned evil and mean, the dresser mirror reflected shadows, and the space under my bed seemed rife with all manner of unknown dark forces. Before going to bed, Dad would always check under my bed, dispel shadows from my closet and line up the stuffed animals to watch over me while I slept. And although Mom would do everything like Dad, it was her impatience, her brusqueness with the ritual, that couldn't quite shake the unease that I felt during that time between twilight and slumber.

For a long time after my dad left, I just wanted to escape the brown floral-walled kitchen with all of his designs hanging up. The shadow box he had made from coffee beans and white kidney beans before all the coffee shops sprouted up and made those things ubiquitous. The teapot and the two-flower glazed-ceramic holders. The brown-and-orange-striped velvet couch he had picked out that went perfectly with these paintings of shadowy, mud-colored people hunched together, which had been given to him by a fellow artist. His painting of daffodils was my favorite. He was everywhere in this house but nowhere in our lives.

I ran away to Madeleine L'Engle's *A Wrinkle in Time*, Carol Ryrie Brink's *Caddie Woodlawn* and Lucy Maud Montgomery's *Anne of Green Gables*, and my brother AWOLed to his room. I would try to gauge what Theo was thinking about, but he became a master at hiding. I can still picture him with his hands in the pockets of the jeans my mom would threaten to throw out, ripped and frayed so they were barely memories of a pair of dark Levis. At some point he added a skull-and-crossbones earring to his look, which Mom lamented over as he walked either into his bedroom or out the front door to meet up with a buddy about painting the set for a musical at school. Probably the best thing to happen to my brother was theater. It gave his feet a place to stay, a place to belong. I wondered to where my mom escaped? She must have wanted to run away to the circus, to a

Serbian folk dance troupe touring Pocatello, Idaho, and Hershey, Pennsylvania, and Frederick, Maryland. Mom began to take us to see folk dances. She seemed to like the "Klompendans" or "Folkloristisch" clogging. In fact, once Dad left, she became interested in many new things—skiing, travelling and clog-dancing—and gave up sewing, doubles tennis and bridge club.

Every family has that wall...the obligatory wall of photos portraying a happy, shiny family. Where you can't see that the father is torn between two very different lives, the mother wondering if she should have studied something else, the son wishing his slingshot was a BB gun, and the daughter hating family photos because she resembles no one. Our photos hung in the family room, right above the TV to the left of the fireplace. They hung long after the happy and shiny left our family. A family of five—a mom, a dad, a boy, a girl and a collie mix. I used to stare at that wall, examine each photo and wonder if the moment captured was real and if the people who weren't in the photo still existed. There were no photos of me prior to being five. For some reason, there were no photo ops available in an orphanage in Korea back in the late '60s. I guess they didn't want any pictures of dirty, lice-ridden children with bloated stomachs and weird bacterial skin diseases. Sometimes it felt like I hadn't existed until the photo where I'm wearing a long pink nightgown to my toes with a white paper flower in my hair. It was my favorite nightgown. I wore it until the white lace at the hem hung way off and began to get caught in my big toe and, once it came up to my knees, my mom began to use it as a floor rag. I think my dad had worked on those photos, framing and arranging them just so, selecting each picture to tell a story of how complete we were. There was a photo of my dad, 13 months old, getting a bath in a copper bathtub, the same one used for my brother's 13-month-old bath photo more than a quarter century later. There was my mother as a fat baby in her silk christening gown and smiling, dimpled cheeks. Dad in his college football uniform in mid-catch. Mom standing next to a giant white gardenia as tall as she in baggy pedal pushers. A photo of my brother with his two crooked front teeth, black square glasses sliding down his freckled nose and his floppy bangs in his eyes. A picture of me at six with two front teeth out and what looked like a dress worn backward. My mom on her wedding day, looking down at her dress, pensively. I wonder if she had an inkling that forever was just a series of photos on the wall. For me, forever was a trio of black-and-white photos with my mom and me playing in autumn leaves. I am wearing a pleated dress with an anchor and my mom is wearing a turtleneck. It was a reminder that we really were that happy family…once upon a time.

I remember our first Christmas tree hunt without Dad—we tried to do things the same way as if he hadn't left. Mom took us to get the Christmas tree at the same place we always got our Christmas tree. Somewhere up past the local swimming pool and tennis courts. When Dad was there, he would hoist me in his arms and trudge up snow banks full of Douglas firs, Fraser firs, blue spruces, eastern red cedar, Scotch pine, Leyland cypress. The choosing would be a three- or four-hour process. Dad had specific qualifications for a tree. He would inspect the needles, check the branches for sturdiness, eye up the circumference, shake the tree at the trunk and walk all around, while Mom would write down the number. Then we would move on to the next one, or Dad would want to look at another set of trees "over yonder." Mom would ask what was wrong with this one. Dad would already be looking at something taller, fuller, younger even. He would make some comment about how "that one looks springier...." I don't think Dad ever found the perfect one. He would have to settle for the next-best thing, as our complaints grew louder and our boots wetter. Theo would pelt Dad with snowballs, aiming for maximum splat effect. Once the decision was made, Dad would chop and saw his own tree down.

Now, Mom dragged us past the same snowy banks with what seemed like the same snow-covered trees. "What about this one?"

Theo shrugged his shoulders.

"I'm cold," I whined.

"It has a nice shape," she said.

"It's not very tall," said Theo.

"Tall's not everything," snapped Mom.

"Fine," said Theo, sticking his hands in his pockets.

"I like this one," I said, pointing to a straggly looking blue spruce. "It looks lonely."

"You mean sickly," Theo said, shaking his head.

Selecting a Christmas tree was sad; what happened to all the trees that didn't get picked? Did they feel inadequate? Were they upset? Or were they happy they got to live another season in the sun with their family and friends? Was Christmastime their holocaust? Where they lost their loved ones, their neighbors?

"This one," Mom said. She shook the tree from the middle and snow fell down.

"It's got a hole on one side," Theo pointed out. "The size of Ohio."

"We can put that section in the corner," Mom insisted. "Plus we can pull some of the top branches down. It'll never show."

"We'll know it's there."

We tagged our tree, and one of the guys at the nursery cut it down. He placed it in our station wagon with the seat down on one side. I sat in the back with the Christmas tree, feeling nauseous the whole 48 minutes it took to drive home. The smell of the pine needles made my mouth fill up with saliva, and no matter how gingerly I swallowed, there was still too much of it in my mouth. I leaned my forehead on the cold windowpane and closed my eyes. I said, "I think I'm going to be sick." I clenched my teeth, trying to hold on, but vaudeville was obsolete and our tap dancing in the hallway was a memory. The nausea came in waves. That car ride became my new standard for emptiness.

After Christmas, my brother got mono and couldn't shake it. For months on end, he sucked on watermelon and green apple Jolly Ranchers and Werther's butterscotch candies. His room smelled of pink, green and tawny-colored hard candies mingled with slightly damp, rumpled bed sheets. I could hear Mom on the phone to her mother and older sister, saying, "I don't think it's just mono. If it were, he'd be up by now. Itching to get out of bed. He's just looking at the window, letting everything go by. Can you blame him? His dad hasn't even called him, and his best friend moved away. I don't know what to do." Mom not knowing what to do always resulted in some change or activity. In this case, it was a new dog. That was just what Theo needed to get out of bed, to go to school, to make new friends.

We drove out past the Christmas tree nursery to a farm where they had a litter of golden retrievers. Since Theo was still feeling sluggish, he bypassed all the rowdy puppies that were climbing on top of each other to get attention and the ones that were wrestling and rolling on the ground. We named her Goldie after he picked the quiet, sleepy-eyed one who was the smallest in the bunch. She was the runt of the litter, and I was sure we were all feeling like her—a little confused and lost amongst all the big dogs and big things in the world.

The thing I feared most back then was that blood really was thicker than water, despite water being persuasive, destructive, warped, especially in a tempest. The universal solvent. That the thing that separates myself from the rest of the family…is it DNA? My brother and my mother are related biologically and it showed, not just in the freckles on the bridges of their noses or moles on the sides of their necks or having the same arm-length-to-body ratio or matching blue eyes. I was adopted when I was five, almost six. Unlike my brother and mom, I do not handle adversity well, or at least with dignity. I railed at everything. I came home and people knew it. Godzilla was a mewling kitty whose eyes were still sealed shut, next to me and my tantrums. School was a landmine of popular kids basking in the glow of their popularity, and less popular kids jostling for position, smart kids figuring out the pecking order of everything, and unpopular kids trying to pretend they didn't mind being unpopular. I wasn't just navigating unpopularity. I was trying to forget I was

Asian, adopted and now from a broken family. I was in constant battle with something, someone, mostly my mom. Of course, later, therapists explained that it was really with…myself. I was a cliché.

I remember the one and only time my brother got angry with me, although I'm sure he was often angry with me but never showed it. It happened on the split-level stairs that led from the living room to the hall entryway. Mom and I were once again screaming at each other, and I'm sure I was spewing words like "I hate you … Nobody understands me … Life sucks in this house … It's no wonder Dad left." And on and on.

My brother walked partway up the stairs so his face was inches from mine, and said, "Why are you such a bitch?"

The one person in the family who never said anything, who never rocked the boat, who put his hands in his pockets, let his bangs cover his eyes and put his head down as the storm raged around him had said something that cut through all the pain. It wasn't that he had said I was a bitch, although I was. It was that he had said aloud that we're all hurt. We're all feeling the same, stop making it worse. This moment did not change things drastically, but it was the first time I realized we were, for better or worse, in this together.

One of my dad's sisters died while I was writing my final paper for a Comparative Literature class at the

University of Pittsburgh. My mom picked me up before I could finish the paper. I was really stuck on how King Lear's life had any impact on me. Aunt Cathy had been my favorite because she had read my melancholy poetry and deemed it poignant and perceptive.

When I was in my early teens, for some reason, I tried to correspond with my dad. I sent him long heartfelt letters and always included some "emo" poems.

> *Your absence created a black hole*
> *Black holes cannot be filled up…*
> *They just can't…*
> *They spin, seemingly, with no light, no sound*
> *The event horizon was your leaving*
> *waiting for your letters*
> *canceled plans because you started a new family*
> *the seasons that changed without new memories*
> *of you*
> *the bicycle that rusted in the garage while*
> *waiting for you*
> *to finish teaching me to ride*
> *the paper dolls you cut years ago from white*
> *transparent paper*
> *discoloring and curling up heavy with time*
> *and dust*
> *shoved under bed in a shoe box that would later*
> *be tossed*
> *in the end glaciers melt*
> *steamboats become obsolete*
> *Atlantis submerges under water*

history is written in rings on trees
galaxies, milky ways explode
universes evolve
but black holes trap matter in...

And matter, dark matter that is, according to some Australian astronomers, weighed 800 billion times as much as the mass of the sun. Scientists claimed that we could see only four percent of the entire universe. If each of us was our own tiny universe...four percent was an immensely shitty small number, and our understanding of each other and even ourselves was just a blip, not even a speck worth dissolving into outer space.

My dad, although artistically creative, didn't know how to respond to this melodramatic prose and poetry, and so he sent them to one of his sisters, the one who had studied English Literature and was a prolific reader. She later wrote to me and told me that my dad had shared my poetry with her, and that she really felt I had talent and encouraged me to continue with it. At the funeral, my mom and I were feeling out of place among my dad's clan. It was an odd feeling...sharing summers together with these people but not really knowing any of them or vice versa. Mom told Dad that Theo couldn't make it to the funeral as he was in a master's program for Technical Theater out-of-state. We had grown up, and I could hear Dad bragging about Theo and his accomplishments, like he had anything to do with them. Then he turned to me and said, "And there's Mandy.... What are you studying at Pittsburgh?" Everyone waited. Just waited, and I realized Dad really didn't know what I was studying at school—that the question was for him alone and not his audience. That it wasn't rhetorical… which he would immediately have followed up with an answer as part of his storytelling. Like all my dad's family, he was gifted with the ability to capture people with words and funny anecdotes that kept growing with each telling.

"Creative Writing and English Literature," I finally said. *Like Aunt Cathy.*

Dad didn't skip a beat. He ignored the awkward silence and resumed bragging about the kids he never saw. Then I had an *a-ha* moment while he started to talk about his other children, the ones he had had with the woman he left us for, that he had to go on. He couldn't look back. It would have been too hard. He hadn't left us because he wanted to but because being responsible for two separate families is a little too much like war. Being left sucks, but being the one to leave…well, I used to think that the prior was the worst….

On the ride back, Mom said, "Your dad put on a few."

I shrugged. "He didn't even know what I was studying!"

"Well, you did change your major a few times," Mom pointed out. "I thought you were going to major in Comparative Literature and Technical Writing?"

"That was you. You were the one who wanted that."

Mom changed the radio station but I wasn't finished. Carole King could shut up. I lowered the volume.

"I always said I was going to be a writer."

"You said this when you were six." Mom fiddled with the car radio as I had accidently bumped the change of station mode. Her tone implied, "It was cute then...."

Carole King began to sing clearer. I closed my eyes and counted to 51, fearful of snapping at my mom like I usually did. Instead I said, "Dad still likes to brag."

Mom settled back into the seat. "Some things don't change." I looked over as Mom began to sing along.

"Nothing really changes," I mumbled.

As Mom tapped on the steering wheel, in sync now with Janis Joplin, it hit me that I was not the only one seeing my dad for the first time in six or seven years. He had been my mom's high school sweetheart, and she had, until recently, all the photos of their lives together hung up on the wall in the family room by the fireplace. It dawned on me then that this was mostly for Theo's and my benefit—a way to never erase that we had shared this past, a way to recognize its loss.

I never did finish the paper. I think I got an incomplete. Something I felt all too well.

I will never know exactly what it took to keep this family of three treading water. If you ask my mom, she shrugs it off. It was just something that had to be done.

If you ask me, we're all treading water. Some are just better at not showing it.

My favorite picture of us is the black-and-white one of you holding my arms in a playful vice-like grip, like you're about to shake a little Shih Tzu. I'm quivering, laughing, gap-toothed. We were raking leaves, or rather, you were, and I was kicking them or jumping into them. You are sporting your usual turtleneck, a big paisley-patterned one in autumn colors, and I have on this navy dress with a big white anchor appliqué on it. The dress is gray in the picture, but I know that it is really navy blue and that the anchor was you. In the picture, you and I have dissolved into giggles.

Time is flexible for **Amanda Roskos**, *like* Yoganidrasana-*pose-flexible, much to her husband's chagrin and, prior to that, her mom's. Immersing herself in yoga kept Amanda from writing for a number of years. She discovered, like time, everything is flexible. Her* namaste *moment happened twice in one fell swoop. With equal amounts of dismay and pride, her twin boys mastered the art of* spinjitzu *time-bending at an early age. They say it is a sign of brilliance…"they" being the parents. These days, Amanda and her family practice the tensile strength of time or, as her husband says, "being late in LaLaLand" (Los Angeles, California).*

WHAT HAPPENED WITH JACOB
Brent C Dill

WE NEVER REALLY TALKED ABOUT IT, but Jacob and I broke up for good that day. I sat on the ground outside his apartment, red-eyed, sniffling and barefoot. An older Asian man was walking by on the way to his apartment, holding his granddaughter's hand. I clutched my English bulldog, Arthur, by his collar as he tried to greet the passersby. His leash was still inside, along with my flip-flops. The man leaned down a little as he passed and silently mouthed, "It's going to be okay."

Most of that day is blurry to me, like a closeup of a watercolor painting, but certain moments are sharper than I can stand. The Asian man's reassurance, his words, might as well have been written on a piece of paper, rolled up, placed in a bottle and thrown into the ocean. That message wasn't for me. But his face stuck in my mind. The granddaughter didn't look at me at all.

One of the two police officers came out of Jacob's apartment carrying some shirts on hangers in crinkly dry-cleaning bags. I stood up halfway, keeping my hand looped into Arthur's collar so he couldn't run away.

"Here are your clothes," the officer said without making eye contact. "You should probably go home."

"Sure," I said, my patience long gone. "Still gonna need my shoes and the leash, though. Can't walk home like this." He remained stoic, but nodded. There was no indication of whose story he believed—mine or Jacob's. I struggled to take the clothes, and he disappeared back into the apartment.

Jacob and I had met online three months earlier. Just a few clicks and Jacob's profile picture, a selfie in the bathroom mirror, was on my screen. He wore a hoodie from the University of Michigan (even though he didn't go to school there). My pic was a group shot cropped down so it was just me leaning to the left with my arm around a mystery. I'm not sure who sent the first message, but it didn't take long before we were talking to each other every day.

We wanted to meet in person, but Jacob was finishing his last weeks of college and I had an internship. We lived on opposite ends of an L.A. freeway. With each exchanged message, the obstacles piled up, but we finally made it work.

That first time I saw him, I immediately felt comfortable with him. Safe. We were supposed to go to dinner, but we just sat in the living room of my apartment and talked. We went from topic to topic without any awkward lulls.

When I asked him about his favorite music, he said, "I really like this one song by the Dixie Chicks." One of my eyebrows shot up. He laughed. "It wasn't a single, so no one's heard it. It's about that person who makes you feel like everything's going to be okay. It's called 'Easy Silence.'"

I looked at him and blinked a few times before getting my laptop to show him the number one most-played song in my iTunes library: "Easy Silence."

After he left later that night, I texted a friend: "I just met someone who's going to be very important in my life. Wow."

A week later, I sat with his family as he graduated from college. Soon after, we visited his parents in Michigan. Then mine in Texas. I drove him to interview for his dream job, and he helped me find an apartment when my lease was up. The whole world changed in those three months. The Supreme Court even made it legal for us to marry in California if we wanted.

But when it all settled down, Jacob started to do some strange things. On several occasions, he invited me over for dinner and wasn't home or answering his phone, even if I arrived at his door only five minutes later. We would make plans with his friends, but they'd get cancelled at the last minute every time. Once, we had a great evening together, eating Italian food and watching movies. Then Jacob just went to bed without even saying goodnight. I sat on the couch in the next room for 30 minutes waiting for him to come back before I went to see what he was doing.

He had excuses: He didn't realize I was coming over for dinner right away. His friends were flaky. He was in adrenal crisis, and I should have given him an emergency dose of cortisone. This last one was a good excuse. He had a congenital condition and couldn't produce the hormones his body needed during stress and trauma. Injuries that were minor to most people could be fatal to him. He had a bathroom counter full of prescriptions, and he always wore a silver medical ID necklace to inform paramedics in cases of emergency. After that, I looked up instructions on how to administer the emergency cortisone on the Internet and memorized them.

A few days before the breakup, he took out the trash and didn't come back. After 15 minutes, I went looking for him. I walked around the apartment complex but couldn't find him. I went down to the parking garage. His car was still in his spot at the end of the row.

The garage was hot, so I decided to go back and wait for him inside. I stopped. I had a nagging feeling in the pit of my stomach, so I walked to his car and tried the handle. Unlocked, but Jacob wasn't inside. That nagging feeling in my gut told me I should pop the trunk, and I listened to it. There he was. Curled up asleep.

I yelled at him. It was the end of July. He easily could have died. Plus, I told him he was treating me like crap and lying to me. He got out of the trunk, dazed. His legs looked like they would give out, so I helped him back to the apartment to get some water.

Later, lying on his bed, I asked if he still wanted to be with me. The air conditioner hummed. Cars honked on the freeway outside. Jacob didn't say anything.

Unable to sit and listen to all the noise, I got up to leave. But I couldn't. I stood at the foot of the bed and stared at him. I wanted him to admit he didn't want to be a couple anymore so it could all end. I needed to hear the words.

"Just say you don't want to be with me," I said.

He started crying. "There's not any sort of future with me," he said, but he wouldn't say why.

Secrets weren't going to cut it. You can't just claim that sort of thing. "If you think—"

"I have a brain tumor," he said. He said he had a growth removed from his brain when he was young. Apparently it was back.

I rallied. I sat down beside him on the edge of the bed. I looked him in the eye and said, "You are the love of my life. I can't believe you thought I would take off because you have a brain tumor."

I kissed him. We cuddled, my mind racing. I felt like I had been the one in the trunk instead of him. He started snoring.

I didn't sleep at all that night.

The morning of the breakup, Jacob called me to take him to the hospital as a precaution because he felt dizzy. We sat there in the emergency room all morning. By the time he saw the doctor, Jacob was annoyed but not dizzy anymore. The doctor couldn't do anything, considering Jacob was fine and well, so it had been a big waste of time.

On the way back to his apartment, Jacob said, "I know things have been hard lately, but you've been such a good boyfriend. I love you."

He was going to shower and walk to my place so we could get lunch. Before he got out of the car, I placed my fingers under his chin and lifted his eyes to meet mine.

"I love you, too, and all I need from you right now is for you to do what you say you're going to do."

He promised.

I sat on the edge of my bed watching TV in my apartment a few blocks away and waited for Jacob to come over. I tried to concentrate on the screen and not watch the clock and worry that he wouldn't show. Then his mother called, not an uncommon occurrence.

"Brent? We just got off the phone with Jacob. He started to slur his words and kind of faded out."

At first I was sure that couldn't be right. After all, I had just been with him. He had just lauded my boyfriendliness. Then I thought about the tumor and quickly agreed to go check on him.

"Oh, good. Because he just told us that you said you never wanted to see him again."

"Umm… What? That's not true. I'll go see what's going on."

Arthur needed to go outside, so I grabbed his leash and threw on some flip-flops. We walked over to Jacob's.

The apartment door was cracked, so I went in. Immediately, I saw Jacob passed out on the kitchen floor and rushed over. I smelled the intense scent of alcohol as I leaned over him to check for breath and beat. Since he was alive and breathing, I kicked off my flip-flops and let Arthur off his leash. Then I got Jacob up and helped him move to the couch.

"Jacob? Jacob?" He was barely answering. "Jacob, babe, I gotta know if you took any pills or what you drank."

"I…I didn't drink anything."

His breath was so thick with vodka that I could have sworn I was in Russia. He passed out again on the couch. I went into his bathroom. On the counter was a gigantic bottle of vodka, half empty.

I poured the rest of it into the sink and went into his closet. There was more hidden booze. I opened at least five large bottles. As I poured everything down the drain, pieces of the puzzle started to fall into place.

Those times he had invited me over for dinner and wasn't there, he was probably in his closet trying to get drunk before I showed up. He was the flaky one, canceling with his friends so he could stay home near his stash. And he didn't need emergency cortisone that night as I sat on his couch waiting for him. No, he'd passed out drunk.

When the last bits of vodka, rum, wine coolers and tequila were gone, I helped Jacob move from the couch to his bed. I sat beside him, staring at my phone. I had to call his mother back. "What am I supposed to tell her?" I asked.

"It doesn't matter what you say to her, she'll always be on my side," he said.

I looked up at him and blinked several times. I didn't know there were sides, much less that we were on opposite ones. I tried to find that safe feeling of easy silence from the night we met, but it was gone.

"Well, I have to call her." I stood up and pressed send.

"No!"

"Carol? Yeah, it's Brent."

Jacob closed his eyes.

"Your son has a serious problem with alcohol. He needs to be in some form of treatment."

All of a sudden, Jacob bolted up and came at me, trying to take my phone. Arthur hurried over and tried to join us by jumping up and playing rough-house, his toenails scratching my legs.

Jacob was a clumsy, messy drunk. He clawed at my face and arms. I held him off with one hand, and I could hear his mother talking through the phone's speaker, even though I had it fully extended in the opposite direction from Jacob. When he realized he wasn't going to get my phone, Jacob shoved me hard into the wall.

As I stood up, he ran around, looking for something. He tore the sheets from his bed and shook them out. He mumbled, but I heard the word "keys."

"You are not leaving."

Slurred response.

"Carol, he's trying to leave," I told her. "No, of course I won't let him."

Abandoning the sheets, Jacob ran out through the living room onto the balcony, which overlooked the freeway. For some reason, I imagined him luring Arthur out there and threatening to throw him off. I told Arthur to stay, and he actually listened, watching me from the doorway of the bedroom as I followed Jacob.

When I looked out around the door frame, Jacob grabbed my arm to pull me onto the balcony so he could run back inside and lock me out. It might have worked if he were stronger, but I latched onto his arm like it was a game of Crack the Whip. I used his momentum to propel both of us back inside and push him all the way up against the wall, face-to-face with me, my forearm pressing his medical ID necklace into his chest.

I still had Carol on the line, so she probably heard me say, "No way, motherfucker," as I immobilized him.

But then he wiggled out and started running around for his keys again. He was yelling, Carol was talking in my ear, and I couldn't see Arthur anywhere.

"Carol? I think I have to call the cops. He tried to lock me on the balcony. He won't stop. If he gets behind the wheel, he'll kill someone."

"You do what you think you have to do," she said. I hung up and dialed 911.

A woman answered. I stood in the middle of the living room and said in a strong voice, "I am involved in a domestic dispute, and I am afraid my boyfriend is a danger to himself and others."

I spotted Arthur. He had jumped up onto the couch, bored of this game he wasn't allowed to take part in. Jacob was in his room, talking. I looked inside.

He had his back to me, his phone to his ear. "I need help," he said to whomever was on the other end of the line. Then he punched himself in the face full force. The back of his head snapped violently toward me, framed by the doorway to his room. That split-second lasted much longer than any split-second has the right to last.

"My boyfriend is beating me," he yelled, as he punched himself again.

I remember thinking, *Wow. How can you hate me so much?*

It was the last time I ever saw him.

"You need to go outside. The police are on their way," said the woman on my phone. I turned away and told her what Jacob was doing, and she paused the call to inform his operator. I heard another punch, a deep, dull thud, but I didn't turn back.

"Come on, Arthur," I said. He jumped off the couch and ran up right beside me, and we walked out, shutting the door and leaving my shoes, Arthur's leash and one seriously sick person still assaulting himself in the apartment behind us.

When I was safely outside, the 911 operator disconnected. I sat down, waiting for the police and holding Arthur by his collar. I had to call Carol. I pressed her name on the call history. She answered and I filled her in. Again, I was methodical and factual, telling her exactly what had happened.

Then Carol asked me some question about Jacob, and I said, "I don't know. I just want to call my mom." And I finally broke down sobbing.

"Soon. Just a little longer," she said without any detectable concern in her voice. In a flash of anger, I shook the phone in front of my face and silently pretended to yell at her. Over the past few months, she had called and texted and called and texted and tried to get me to tell her things her son wouldn't. I had no defense for this level of mothering and scrutiny. When I had talked to Jacob about it, he just laughed and said something about me not being Jewish.

The anger and its energy left as suddenly as it had appeared. I put the phone back to my ear. I slumped against the wall and told Carol I would call her back when I knew something.

The cops came, stern and sterile. After hearing my side of the story, they went in and found Jacob. They came back out to check my knuckles to see if I had been punching anyone. After they saw my knuckles were clear, I told them about Jacob's adrenal condition and said I needed my shoes and the leash from inside so I could go home.

They both disappeared into the apartment again. Ten minutes went by. I considered stepping inside and getting everything myself. But I didn't. I really didn't want to ever set foot in that apartment again. I sat down just outside the door. It was quiet except for the hum from the A/C units that protruded from the windows of each apartment. That's when the Asian man walked by with his granddaughter and offered his silent reassurance.

Moments later, the officer brought me my dry-cleaning instead of the two things I had asked for. I was holding the bags in one hand and Arthur by the other. The crinkling of the bags was loud and scared Arthur, so he kept pulling away, trying to escape. I finally just threw the shirts on the concrete and the crinkling stopped. Arthur sat back down beside me as if nothing had ever happened.

The other cop came outside to stand. He didn't have my shoes or the leash, but he shrugged and tried to make conversation.

"Well, he's very drunk," he said with an odd chuckle of sympathy.

"Yeah."

"How long have you guys been broken up?"

"I'm not sure. How long ago did your partner bring me my dry-cleaning?"

I did eventually get the flip-flops and leash. I called my mom as I walked back to my apartment while crying and wrangling the dog and dry-cleaning. I don't remember a single word my mother said that day, but I remember feeling comforted. We kept talking well after I had gotten home and locked myself in my apartment.

My phone was dying, and there were no convenient wall outlets. They were all behind furniture or too low to the ground. So, I sat on the floor in the dark. I cried and talked to my mom. I cried and worried that Jacob had copied my keys at some point without me knowing. A few hours earlier, I had genuinely believed I would be nursing this man through chemotherapy. Now I was sitting there on the hardwood floor, worried he was on his way over to hurt me or my dog. Overreaction? Maybe. But he had become a completely different person. He wasn't the comfort and safety I had known.

My mom and I stayed on the phone for a long time, even though we mostly sat in silence. It wasn't the type of silence that was searching for words to fill itself. I couldn't stay on the line with her forever, though. I was drained, falling asleep. We said goodbye, but before we hung up, we did the opposite of what cute couples do when they say, "You hang up." "No, you hang up."

The opposite? It's when you both hear the other person start to cry again, quietly at first and trying to hide it. Then you can't control it and you say you love each other, but it's almost incomprehensible through the tears.

And then you both hang up.

I was still sitting on the floor beside my phone when Mike and Carol called. (Yes, Jacob's parents' names were Mike and Carol, like the Bradys.) Carol needed to hear the whole story from the beginning, so I tried to tell it while they interrupted with questions. They asked if he had been acting strange lately.

"He said he had a growth on his brain when he was young, and it was reoccurring, but he hadn't told anyone, yet," I said.

"Can you believe that?" Carol asked Mike.

"Hmm. Brent, Jacob—" Mike started.

Carol spoke over him and finished the news. "Jacob never had any sort of growth on his brain."

The lie stung, not just because of all the anguish I'd been through worrying about Jacob's health, but also because it showed me that Jacob was done with the relationship and just didn't want to tell me. After all, he would have had to eventually either admit the lie or get cancer to cover it up.

Then Carol added, "I told him on Wednesday that maybe he shouldn't be in a relationship right now."

She had been telling her son to break up with me. Did she think I was making things worse? Wednesday happened to be the day of the trunk fiasco. If it weren't for me, she probably would have gotten a phone call even less pleasant than that afternoon's.

I told her I thought Jacob might be seriously mentally ill and needed help.

"What would you have us do, Brent? Please. Tell us since you seem to know."

Just as I thought I was going to get off the phone and rest, a good friend of Carol's who was a psychologist joined the conversation. I was asked to tell the story again. I did, only this time I ended it with, "And after today, Carol, I don't want to speak to you or your son ever again."

For the first time, I was happy the cops had given me my dry-cleaning. I wouldn't ever need to make contact with Jacob or his family ever again. I wouldn't realize until a week later that the shirts in the bags weren't even mine.

Then Carol asked me if I would be willing to pick her up at the airport the next day because she was flying in to collect Jacob and take him back to Michigan with her.

"Get a fucking taxi."

Man, I wish I had really said that. I didn't. I just

said no, hung up and fell asleep on the floor next to my phone with Arthur resting his chin on my hip.

I didn't dream of the reassuring Asian man. I didn't have dreams full of deep, dull thuds. And I didn't dream about Jacob closing his eyes just after I put the phone to my ear.

I dreamed about swimming in a small, sunny lagoon with my friends from college and our families. We were cleaning the lagoon, I think, but we were also watching a movie on a huge screen that rose out of the water and extended up into the sky beyond what I could see. And even though we were all laughing, there was no sound. Just a bright quiet that rested over us. There was a big tree in the middle of the lagoon. It had gigantic tropical leaves on the ends of too-small branches. The leaves were so big that they weighed down the branches until each vast leaf barely skimmed the surface of the water.

It was peaceful.

"Easy Silence" is still my favorite song. I don't even think of Jacob when I listen to it. But when the easy silence isn't there, my mind still wanders back to those too-sharp moments. The sound and smell of pouring a full bottle of tequila down the drain, the crinkling of dry-cleaning bags and listening to myself use the words "domestic dispute." Every time I remember them, those things are vividly the same as they were that afternoon. But when I see Jacob framed in that doorway with his back to me, hitting himself in the face, I don't see a person filled with hate. I don't see someone who was mentally ill or a good-for-nothing drunk. I just see a guy who was scared and running out of options.

 **Brent C Dill** *would fall in love with a mop in a top hat if it told him he were clever. He grew up in Texas, but his constant need for reassurance and approval led him to Los Angeles. He would rather make you laugh than make you cry, but he would rather make you cry than have you stare at him in indifference. If he could invite five people to a fantasy dinner party, he would invite Allison Janney, J.K. Rowling, Aaron Sorkin, Natalie Maines and an oddly formal mop he just met. Brent lives in Pasadena, California, with his English bulldog, Arthur.*

FORTY-FIFTH REUNION

Susan Martin

So Grovers, let's get together for the greatest rally, ever, our Forty-fifth Reunion. See you the weekend of June 3.

> *Yours always,*
>
> *Steffie Reinbold Adams*
> *Class Agent*

I READ THE LETTER, STUFFED IT BACK in the envelope filled with information about the reunion and tossed it in the wastepaper basket. Forty-five years after graduation, Pine Grove College was more than a memory. It was an embarrassment I would rather forget.

How right it had seemed back then. I had applied there, and to other schools just like it, because my family told me that was what I wanted. They said I was a dreamer, a scholar. I belonged in an all-female institution set in a provincial town. I could only grow, learn and dream, they insisted, in an atmosphere of a million daisy-chain traditions, and rules and regulations based on Old Testament law. I had been indoctrinated in the theory that "Mother knows best," and so I simply went along with this line of thinking. It never occurred to me to choose any path other than the one of least resistance. Rebellion was unheard of.

Oh, yes, it was ideal for me. It was the only girls' school within a radius of 20 miles, and within that area there were two all-male colleges and an all-male university. We were 450 virgins among 12,000 horny men who were willing to do anything to get us to go to bed with them, even marry us. And to that end, the faith-based college worked to our advantage.

Life then, in the late '50s, was very simple. At age 18, young ladies were officially placed on the marriage block. We had four years in which to achieve the ultimate goal of matrimony. We all strove to reach this goal, for such was the success of the indoctrination. We had been trained by our mothers to be perfect housewives—how to select china, how to grow roses, how to be the perfect hostess. To this end, the college continued our education. Freshman orientation included using hand cream on our chapped heels. "Gracious living" was taught and practiced on Sundays and Wednesdays. The unwritten mission of the college was not just to get its girls married, but married to the "right" man. It became a question of who you married, because a real woman was exactly that—who she married.

Too soon after graduation, it was the '60s. The harsh realities of those times served as a pin to break the plastic bubble that surrounded our little world. Our nation was at war over the fate of a country most of us had never heard of or cared about. My cousin Joe told his mother that if he were drafted, he would run away to Canada. His mother said, "Do it!" The African-American community became articulate and sometimes violent in their demands for equal rights. In the face of now-acceptable rebellion, all we had striven to achieve as young women just a few years before became and remained trivial and irrelevant. I couldn't go back to that, not even for a weekend.

Two weeks after I received the invitation to the reunion, I went into the city on an errand for my husband. After completing this, I went into a coffee shop to have lunch. A young man held the door open for me. I started to go for an empty seat at the end of the counter. "Here, hon," the waitress said to me as she indicated a seat near the door. "He's leaving. You can take his seat. Save yourself the walk." She was referring to my obvious incapacitation caused by corrective surgery on my left foot. It had not been a serious procedure, but it nevertheless required that my foot be encased in a walking cast.

I ordered my lunch, and while I waited for it, I looked around at the other people sitting at the U-shaped lunch counter. I was startled as I saw across from me at the counter, across 35 feet and 45 years, my college advisor, Professor Heinrich.

I remembered how I had fallen in love with Professor Heinrich on that first day of my junior year at The Grove when I had gone to see him about a schedule change. He was new to the college then. There was an aura of vitality about him that seemed to send out vibes of energy, and a nimbus of sexuality surrounded him. A short man, his slightly bulbous nose and receding chin gave him an impish look. He was dressed in gray pants and a white shirt that was open at the neck, and he had rolled his sleeves up to his elbows, not the usual professorial gear.

Warm and effusive in his greeting, he spoke as though it were a given that we shared a mutual love of English literature. "My specialty really is American literature," he said. "I wrote my doctoral dissertation on Melville. I love the truth of Americans. They seem to be disciples of Shakespeare. Do you like Shakespeare?" That was when I knew we were going to embark together on a fantastic journey, as he taught and I learned. Feeling more like an idiot every minute, I stumbled and blushed my way through the interview.

When I left his office, I ran to the snack bar where I triumphantly announced to my group of friends, "Wait till you see the chairman of the English Department. He's just what this place needs." When they met him later on, they reacted the same way I had.

After that, it seemed as though the entire college was engaged in a love affair with Professor Heinrich. The girls lingered after class to talk to him. They went over to his table in the snack bar to join him for coffee. They found any excuse to be with him or at least in his presence. Professor Heinrich returned this adoration in the love he declared for the college. "No politics," he said. The college administrators, too, loved Professor Heinrich. He could move and shake his department without moving and shaking the establishment.

A book of poetry he had written was being sold in the college bookstore. Many of my friends bought it and, with giggles, asked him to autograph their copies. I looked through the book but I couldn't get myself to buy it. His poetry was in the "Beat" style of the time, a style that I felt somehow bypassed the genuine poetic experience.

But he was my Professor Heinrich, and in his professional role I loved him truly. I lived for his Shakespeare course and doted on every word he said. Just as I had fallen in love with Professor Heinrich at first sight, I had fallen in love with Shakespeare six years before, when I had read the first pages of *The Merchant of Venice* for high school freshman English. Professor Heinrich didn't just teach Shakespeare. With the energy that was so much a part of him, he made it live. With every explanation of language, usage, plot and characterization, Shakespeare became an integral and necessary part of my life. Professor Heinrich read passages out loud, playing all the characters' roles. When he did *Macbeth*, I really did see a dagger before me, and with his perfect presentation, oh, did I ever identify with poor parent-manipulated Ophelia in her mad scene.

It was beyond me how someone who could send a class of 20-year-old girls into a tailspin with his comments on "Oh, she doth teach the torches to burn brightly" could possibly write poetry that trivialized the entire genre.

During the summer vacation of my junior year, I lived on the glow of my infatuation with Professor Heinrich. I was too shy and embarrassed to share this with anyone, but my mother commented that I managed to find something wrong with every boy I dated. "Just who or what are you looking for?" she demanded. "Is there someone or something I should know about?" I couldn't wait to get back to school in September. But when I got there, things were different. Professor Heinrich went around campus with a small clique he had formed of young faculty members. For some reason, the serenity of our campus was beginning to crack. There seemed to be factions, sides and issues. Rumors abounded about grants and their distributions. It seemed as though every department in the college was fighting over pennies. Professors were at war with each other over promotions and salaries. Students were being involved, as faculty members tried to get Student Government to take sides. The dean of the college gave it a name: *politics*.

One evening as I was leaving the dorm to go to play rehearsal, the receptionist stopped me. "There's a telegram here for Professor Heinrich," she said. "It came here by mistake. On your way to the theater, could you drop this off at his office?"

"Sure," I replied. Play rehearsals had been rough. We were doing *The Trojan Women*, and in deference to the tragedy of ancient Troy, our director had us rolling around on the floor a lot. I was wearing my rehearsal outfit—sweat shirt, Bermuda shorts and a pair of Keds, all of which I had destroyed in the prop room.

I went up to his office and knocked on the door. He opened it and appeared delighted to see me. "I knew someday you would come," he said.

He knew some day I would come? I asked myself. *Why would he expect me?*

He looked at me in a way to indicate that, among all the girls, I was very special to him. It was the warm smile and a soft expression in his eyes. A feeling of complete confusion born out of inexperience filled me. I struggled with conflicting emotions—pride that I was his "chosen," puzzlement as to why (for I was no great beauty), embarrassment at being caught in the grungiest of all getups.

"Sit down," he said. "I'm working on a new collection of poetry, and I want you to hear some of my work." I obediently sat down and tried to find something in the room to look at to hide my confusion. He kept reading one poem after another to me, each one replete with references to colors and ending with a rhetorical question. None of them made too much sense. I kept my eyes downcast. They wandered past the paint and glue spots on my Bermuda shorts to the holes in my worn-out Keds. I blushed for both of us.

As he waited for me to succumb to the magic of his words, I looked at him and watched him in disbelief. There was something so pathetic about his trying to gain my approval or admiration for his attempt at poetry. For the first time, I realized he was two inches shorter than myself. "Professor," I said as I rose from my chair and started for the door, "I'm late for play rehearsal."

Later in the year, it became evident that he was having an affair with one of my classmates, Jane St. Claire. She was a brilliant student, and she also wrote poetry. I could have been almost jealous if it were not for the fact that they were seen hanging out at all the student spots in town together. It was too disappointing. He still was a saint in my imaginary shrine, and I didn't want my special professor to be just another one of the kids.

Margaret England, the girl in our crowd who always seemed to be able to get the inside dope on everything, reported to us that she heard from a cousin of hers, who knew Professor Heinrich from before he came to The Grove, that he had had an affair with a student in his last position. That's why he was asked to leave, and that was it. The feet of clay of my college idol, just another guy trying to get laid. I did have to give him credit, though, for his novel approach.

A year after graduation, my parents announced with love, pride and relief my engagement to Norman Green. Norman had graduated from one of the men's colleges near Pine Grove and had settled in the town. Before we were married, we took a sentimental tour of our respective campuses. As we walked through The Grove Ad Building, I felt irresistibly drawn to the English offices. I took Norman to meet Professor Heinrich. He was warm and cordial to Norman and congratulated us both. "She's a special person," Professor Heinrich told him. "Always be gentle with her."

Yet the meeting was again a disappointment to me. He told us he was leaving The Grove. He couldn't stand the politics, he said, and the ridiculous finishing-school traditions of the place got on his nerves. "The worst has to be *Date With Dad Weekend*," he said in total disgust. I indicated that I understood why a poet of his exquisite sensitivity would have to leave a place whose outstanding social event of the year was *Date With Dad Weekend*.

Still, Norman noticed a certain look of adoration on my face. It gave me a special glow that he had never seen before. He understood that I had some special feelings there.

On my part, it was now little more than an idealized memory of my relationship with a brilliant teacher. It was Professor Heinrich he who had given meaning and purpose to my four years at The Grove. As for the humanity of his sexual needs and desires, well, any girl at The Grove could tell you, "Boys will be boys." I tried to explain this to Norman, but he always remained a little bit jealous.

Two years after we were married, I began graduate work at the nearby university, which did accept women on the graduate level. I stopped by the Pine Grove bookstore to buy index cards and notebooks. There on a clearance shelf were copies of Professor Heinrich's book of poetry. They were on sale for $2. The torch still burned, though not so brightly. With the inducement of bargain-basement prices, I finally broke down and bought a copy.

Now, 45 years later, Professor Heinrich and I found ourselves on the verge of meeting again. He hadn't changed much at all. Although what was left of his hair was snow-white and although his face was lined and wrinkled, he remained a well-aged version of his old self. As he drank his coffee, he seemed preoccupied, as though he were composing a poem. He didn't recognize me.

I debated with myself as to whether or not I should say hello to him. "What would we say to each other?"

I asked myself. I would ask him what he's doing, and he would likely tell me that he had retired from his last college, relieved that he no longer had to deal with politics. Next he would tell me that he had written another volume of poetry. Then he would ask me what I was doing, and I would tell him about my children, my teaching career, community involvement—my lifetime in five minutes.

My foot began to throb. I looked down at the cast. It looked clumsy and stupid. Once again, just as when I had delivered the telegram to him all those years ago, my foot gear was not suitable for a meeting with Professor Heinrich. I paid my check, left a tip and limped out of the coffee shop.

When I got home that night, I took out my copy of Professor Heinrich's book. I opened it to the first page. I couldn't get myself to turn to page two. I put it away and took out my *Complete Works of Shakespeare*. I turned to the sonnets. The pages were covered with markings. Red ink indicated my own underlinings and comments. Blue ink indicated what Professor Heinrich had said on the subject during lecture, his words that made Shakespeare live for me. My favorite sonnet had always been 130. It had always seemed as though it were written for me:

> *I love to hear her speak, yet well I know*
> *That music hath a far more pleasing sound;*
> *I grant I never saw a goddess go,*

My mistress, when she walks treads on the ground.
And yet, by heaven, I think my love as rare
As any she belied with false compare.

And then the professor's explanation, putting into words which before had only been a feeling: "Shakespeare brings enrichment into our lives, not by creating an impossible, unreachable sublime, but by showing us the sublime that exists in ourselves, just as we are."

As I read, I was transported back to The Grove campus. I was gossiping and giggling with the girls in the snack bar, reliving the agonies of the fall of Troy in the theater and doting on every word a professor I adored said in a class I loved. I was a girl again. For one more time in my life, I was safe and happy in a world of halls covered with plastic ivy. That was my 45th reunion.

**Susan Martin** *took delight in her 32-year career as a high school English and creative writing teacher. Now she takes delight in having passed the torch to her young successors and giving them the opportunity to "teach the torches to burn bright." When she is not reading or writing, she and husband Frank take advantage of the many opportunities for enjoyable retirement at the New Jersey shore and nearby New York City. An inveterate beach bum, she is at the shore and in the ocean almost every summer day. She is a member of the Jersey Shore Poets. See them on Facebook.*

MERCY

Michael Moran

SHE WAS MY CONSTANT. Shiny and bright at the beginning of the evening, darker later on. Hell, more than seven years later, I still think about her each day. How she filled me with confidence, how she took my hand and pulled me away from all of the pain of the past. How she became the lover that seduced me and held me tight. Even before the first taste of the day, when I held her, I started to salivate. My heart raced and my chest tightened. As her cold liquid poured down my throat, I felt the tight coil inside of me start to loosen. It felt so good. Each day, for 25 years, I felt that.

Alcohol. God, I loved her.

My great-grandparents on my father's side were drunks. They were the type of drunk you would find in an alley or a shelter. The story goes that they gave up my grandmother as an orphan to the convent until her brother was old enough to take care of her. My father inherited the trait, and though functional early on in his marriage and while my older brother was young, he consistently put himself and his home life in jeopardy. He got sober the year I was born, and in the 39 years we shared, I only saw him relapse twice and for a total of three weeks. While my brother has seemingly dodged the bullet, I was not so lucky, and from the first moment that I put Alcohol to my lips, I knew that I could free myself from all of the junk inside my head, that I was home.

I was in sixth grade when we first met. I was a ball of fear for as long as I could remember. As a small child, I loved to play outside in our suburban neighborhood. It was a great place to grow up, but with my father trying to stay sober and restart his business and my mom popping her "mother's little helpers" (prescription, of course), I had very little in the way of guidance and structure in my home life. This left me free to explore and play by myself until, one afternoon, when I was six years old, a neighbor took me into his basement and forced me to do sexual acts. He continued to abuse me for a summer, maybe more, and each time it would end with the threat that if I told anyone, he would kill my family. Six years old! Where was my mother? Who was keeping watch over me? When it stopped I was thankful, but I realized that the God that I was being raised to pray to had not saved me. He had not stepped in when my parents, doing the best they could, I suppose, failed to protect me. So one day, when I was 12, I met Alcohol in my friend's basement. Knowing what it did to my mother and knowing that my father didn't touch it because it got him in trouble, I stole a bottle of vodka.

When I was 16, I was arrested with a bunch of friends. It was a house party, and I guess it got too loud and the neighbors called the cops. I was too messed up to run, and they took five of us down to the station. They called our parents and wrote us citations, and then left us in a cell. My father came and didn't say a word. When the time came, he paid my fine and still never said a word. I wasn't punished. My mother said some things under her breath for about a week after, but the message was clear to me that my father had been there and he wanted to help me. I see now just how much that hurt.

Early in my 20s, the romance intensified. Alcohol and the ritual surrounding her became all I lived for. I was a smart but mediocre student who could get decent grades just by showing up. And since going to class wasn't conducive to staying up all night in bars, showing up was really all I did. Alcohol became so important that most everything was left by the wayside. A varsity football player in high school, my weight climbed to unhealthy numbers. I was barely six feet tall and weighed close to 340 pounds. The self-loathing that had taken seed from the abuse as a child had grown into full-blown self-hatred. I could barely look in the mirror. I only felt centered when I was numb. I was destructive and careless. The burden of my past was eclipsed by the rippling rush of Alcohol.

There are so many stories to tell about Alcohol, about our love. There was a night when, after working until 11 p.m., I drank while driving to the club and then proceeded to drink even more. I was having a great night and when the bar closed, I drove through town to get to my apartment on the other side. I stopped on that cold night at an ATM in the heart of a risky part of the city to withdraw money, with the intention of buying food at an all-night convenience store near my home. Snow had started to fall, and after getting some money out, I crawled back into my truck. It was so warm in the cab and the windows had fogged up. One of my favorite songs had come on the radio and I decided that, just for a minute, it would be okay to close my eyes and listen to it. Three hours later, I woke to the sound of metal pinging against my foggy window. When I rolled it down partway, I saw a cop with his flashlight shining right at my face. I was so startled that I didn't know what to do. He asked me how long I had been there, and I said about three hours. I told him that I had worked a double and had stopped for a few beers, decided that I would just sit until I could drive and must have drifted off. He asked if I was okay and then said he'd let me go if I allowed him to follow me home.

That wasn't the only time the police caught Alcohol and me together. There was the time I was arrested in broad daylight in a public park for public indecency and lewd behavior. And there was the time that I blacked out in a more wooded part of the city and slammed my truck off the curb, blowing both tires on the right side of my truck. My father rescued me that night, too.

The saddest moment of my life occurred because of my love of Alcohol, and I still cry inside each time I think about it. I am still so damned ashamed.

After getting a DUI, my father arrived early in the morning after my arraignment at the county jail to take me to get my truck out of the pound. While waiting and due to the stress of it all, my father went into congestive heart failure and had to be rushed to the hospital by ambulance. It was my fault, and yet he said nothing. Maybe he felt that my sins were his sins. Maybe he felt he was to blame for my actions. He was wrong. I was a grown man. I needed to stand by myself and deal with the consequences of my actions. He continually co-signed for my bullshit and I let him. How I wish I had those decisions back to make over again.

My relationship with Alcohol was clearly out of hand. My ego was limitless. I was insane. I was reckless to the point of hurting someone, yet this love affair raged on. We met every night, and even though with each date I grew less satisfied, I still crawled back to her time and time again.

My health went unchecked for years. I had been diagnosed as a type 2 diabetic in my early 30s but was never interested in monitoring or controlling my blood sugar, especially if it meant that I must give up the love of my life. Eight years later, I got a blister on my foot that developed over time into a sore that wouldn't heal. That sore became infected. I continued to ignore it until, one day, when I was woken up by the screams of my girlfriend. It was July 3 and she had just returned from a trip to gather her possessions from her old place, which she had shared with her ex-boyfriend in another state. I didn't know it at the time, but she was cheating on me, which just further proves the denial I was in about my reality and just how much I was in love with Alcohol.

She screamed because it was the middle of the day, and there I was lying in bed, the sheets soaked from fever, my left foot exploded. The room smelled of infection, and I sat up, still in a daze. Mad from being jostled from the peace of being practically unconscious, I stared at her. She was yelling at me that I needed to go to the hospital and that she was calling an ambulance. Deliriously, I told her to calm down and that I would not go if I had to be put on a stretcher, but that if she took me I would.

I was 39 years old. I was barely making a living as a freelance graphic designer and I had no insurance. I remembered what my father had said when he was sick and needing to go to the hospital. He said to my mother,

"Ginny, take me to see the nuns. They will always take care of us. Take me to Mercy." That stuck in my head. I felt so sick that I wanted to die. My foot was gangrenous, and my blood poisoned by infection. I was septic and I was dying.

The first night in Mercy Hospital was a blur, with a priest giving me last rites, my girlfriend angrily looking on, and my brother and his wife sitting in the shadows. I rolled on my side and faced out the window and said to whatever I thought God was at the time, "I will not pray to you. You did not protect me as a small child, and I have lived in constant fear. I will not fear you. If I do not wake up, that is fine with me. See you on the other side of nothing."

Twenty hours later, I was missing three toes. Time became fluid. Days trickled by in 10-minute intervals, just like the morphine drip that was suspended above the trauma below my knee. I had surgery two days later to remove most of my left foot. Five days on from that horror, they took what was left of the foot and much of my lower leg, halfway up my shin. Throughout this time, in a druggy haze, I saw my mother and brother and many of my friends, but not my girlfriend. She had come to me between the second and third surgery and said that she had not signed up for this, that she was leaving me to go tour Japan with her ex-boyfriend's band. It was all just so surreal. I stayed in the hospital another 39 days, healing and learning how to take care of myself. I can honestly say that, in that time, the only thing I thought about was what had gotten me to that place in my life.

Throughout this whole ordeal, even while in the hospital, I always felt hopeful. Maybe that's the positive side of denial, and most likely delusional, but for all of the darkness that followed me, I never once thought I would die. I didn't ever think that this was the time that I would just let go, wallow in self-pity and sit back and let my health fade. I never once thought that I couldn't or wouldn't right the ship, but I certainly had no idea how that was going to happen. Perchance it was my father's spirit in me that propped me up. I'd like to think it was. I felt loved. My friends continued to visit and stay with me. So many people sent their love and healing thoughts. This was a love that I could understand, not the religious love I felt so abandoned by.

One day, I was lying in my hospital bed and my brother stopped by. He told me of a tattoo he saw in a movie about a sea captain. It was a hand tattoo. He and I often talked about tattoos, and it was an easy subject to discuss during such a difficult time. He told me that he saw it as the first mate struggled on deck during a storm. In the end, he had to grab onto the rail with both hands and hold on for his life. When he did that, you could see across his knuckles the words "HOLD FAST." A day later, a friend of mine in the music business came to visit and gave me a CD by a new band called Hold Steady.

Two weeks later, I started reading a memoir by a man whose life was a total mess, and his story was about his path to recovery. A friend had given it to me and implored me to get into recovery once I left the hospital. He told me that he and his wife truly thought that I was dying and needed to change my life. Initially, I pushed back on starting the book because I didn't want their lecture or their message, and I certainly did not want to let my mind drift to their picture of me dying or dead. But I picked up the book because I felt, much like the author, that I was living a life that was completely unmanageable, even while feeling completely invincible at the same time. I quickly became engrossed, and in the last half of the book, the writer shared his desire to escape from a court-mandated rehabilitation facility. An unlikely person took the time to sit and truly talk with him about recovery and how it asked that he simply (but not so easily) hold on for just another day, or hour or minute, if need be. It was when I read that sentence that I connected the dots.

Hold fast. Hold steady. Hold on.

These phrases formed the groundwork for a mindset to do the hard work of getting fitted with a prosthetic leg and learning to walk again.

Two months out of the hospital, I was barely getting around. The nerve pain was incredible. It felt like lightning shooting through my leg every 40 seconds. I had the usual phantom pain where I would feel my left toe or ankle hurt even though the limb had been removed, but the nerve pain was something different. It came and went, but I never knew when or for how long it would stay. And it was that pain, after not drinking for almost four months, that brought me back to Alcohol. The lure of numbing myself physically was no different from the psychological pull of wanting to feel no emotional pain, and I knew just how to do that. Double shots of chilled vodka. They say that when an alcoholic starts to drink again after not drinking for a period of time, they start right back where they were. That appeared to be true with me. My tolerance was high and I drank hard.

My mind was so shattered by the loss of my limb that I was barely holding it all together. I could not focus enough to work a job in my field, so I got a job as a cashier at a market that was close enough to my home that I could walk to work. I couldn't drive due to bilateral nerve damage that caused tremors in my remaining foot. For a time, my life revolved around working and drinking. Then I added another element into the equation. I met someone, and we both were so badly damaged from our pasts that we clung to each other. We drank together, and we reveled in our survival and we loved each other as best we could, but the truth was that I wasn't surviving. Not really. I had no real job, I did not have insurance, and this woman was not going to let me drag her down.

We broke up after two years. She had been my rock, helping me to physically heal from the amputation, and I offered her love and attention, but that was not enough, especially since my first love, Alcohol, was more important to me. I drank every day. I could not see ahead any further than survival mode would let me. Desperate to win her back, I came to believe that what I needed was a good job, insurance and, excuse the pun, to be able to stand on my own two feet. Knowing that my father had found his answer in sobriety, I decided that this was the best way to get those things and prove myself to be worthy of her love.

I called a friend of my ex who I knew had gotten sober and asked her to meet me. I told her my story, and she told me hers. I cried and cried like a baby that summer evening on the bleachers of a Little League baseball field near my house. She asked me if I could stay sober until the following afternoon when she would meet me at a 12-step meeting. I said yes, but I couldn't do it. Alcohol and I got together later that evening. But the next day I *did* meet her, and it was at that meeting that I heard a reading, a list of promises that would come to fruition if I would give of myself to recover from my addiction. And it was that reading that kept me sober that night, and it was that same reading that led me to go to my next meeting the following day.

I didn't know what I was doing, and often I lapsed into tears, feeling paralyzed by fear, but I kept going back. I felt better being there than I did at home. I was around people who understood and did not judge. I was able to start to listen and hear in others' words my own story. My struggle was not as unique as I thought it was.

I surrendered because I was sick and tired of feeling so sick and tired, and when I did this, I began to find in my heart something bigger than my love for Alcohol. I found the ability to start to love and respect myself just a bit. I listened and discovered that if I followed the suggestions of others who'd broken up with her, I might just find a new life for myself.

As I strung one sober day into two, and two into a week, and a week into a month, and months into years, my sense of self gave me the chance to make better decisions and to find pride in the moment, to feel love for my present life. I learned how to forgive myself. I learned how to connect with my Higher Power. A power that was not the God of my childhood—that Biblical, smiting, bearded old man—but a spirit or sense of community, of a collection of energy and of the universe. I learned that we are all threads in the fabric of humanity, and that each one of us has an important role and a responsibility to help each other.

I still feel her grip, Alcohol's, all these years sober. I see the look in my wife's eye when she has a second glass of wine, or the way my best friend's laughter loosens while drinking beer at a concert or a baseball game, and I want to be right there beside them, the tautness gone from my chest and replaced by the calm that comes soon after the first sip. But I have learned that you can choose between a love that destroys you and one that builds you up. I am blessed to have survived the first to live now in the light of the second.

**Michael Moran**, *graphic designer and visual artist, never wanted to be bald—but just ended up that way. A natural and engaging public speaker, he has spoken at conferences sharing his journey from last rites to recovery and purpose. He has had roles in several movies including* The Road, *has had artwork exhibited in group shows and is a singer in a rock-n-roll band. A native of Pittsburgh, Michael lives in Forest Hills with his wife and stepdaughter, and soon a golden retriever, once he gets a bigger yard. He has been clean and sober for eight years.*

THE INVITATION
Jodi Teti

ALTHOUGH I DIDN'T TRULY UNDERSTAND the horror of 13 until well into my adult years, I got a glimmer of it in seventh grade. Fourteen days before the end of the school year, to be precise. The day I failed to receive The Invitation.

Ten months prior to that, the summer before my 13th year, my best friend was Maggie Graham. We met at a slumber party midway through the sixth grade over *Light as a Feather, Stiff as a Board*. In this game, everyone crowded around a chosen girl who would lie on the floor, eyes closed. We all slid two fingers under the prone body, chanting "light as a feather, stiff as a board," until we could "feel" the body begin to levitate. Maggie and I, abnormal cells in the organelle of teendom, were both disdainful of the fear it invoked in the other girls.

Our simpatico was new to me. I was never what you might call popular, though there were vague gestures toward it. I was invited to play soccer during recess in the fourth grade. Soccer was the game of choice. This probably had to do with the fact that Harry Sprott, the best-looking boy in school, championed its play. Also, I was cute in a wholesome, farm-girl sort of way. That gave me a certain cachet in the romantic department, including ascendance into holding hands with one of the boys of the in-crowd on top of the tire tower during recess.

But near the end of sixth grade, I snubbed the wrong girl. Cathy Chickering had a chin like an acute triangle and was as chatty as her name betokened. She wasn't mean, just nice. Inclusively nice, when I wanted to be her only friend. The effect of my having a twin brother, I suppose, I was always pushing for intense, two-person relationships.

Cathy balked when I asked her to limit her friendship to just me. Stung, I told her she wasn't good enough to be my friend. The story got out to the sixth-grade class, and I was shunned. Shunning consisted of sitting against the wall during recess and reading books while everyone else played soccer. If the playground was a Native American village, I was a known carrier of smallpox, quarantined on its edge.

Looking back on it, I certainly behaved badly toward Cathy, whom I convicted of the crime of not wanting to enter into a friendship of exclusivity at the age of 12.

Her punishment, however, couldn't rival mine. I wasn't even able to join the reject girls perfunctorily playing four square in the blocked-off street. For a month, I sat against the wall and read, pretending that I was enjoying myself. Even my twin brother ignored me.

I was alone, until the day Maggie left the soccer game and asked if I wanted to join her on the swings. I did.

I fell in love with Maggie that day, kicking our feet into the sky and laughing. The playground shaming fell away and, for the first time in a long time, I played during recess. Played without worrying about the swirl of social agenda around me. That weekend, I slept over at Maggie's house, and our friendship was cemented when we stole into the kitchen and shared a plastic tub of Cool Whip while watching *The Outer Limits* on television.

Maggie's friendship yielded many benefits. Her family consisted of four people; mine had eight. This meant she had Cheerios, not Tasteos, for breakfast. At lunch her treat was a Butterfinger. Mine, when it came at all, was a four-for-a-dollar "mountain bar," thick globules of waxy chocolate shot through with peanuts surrounding a milky, grainy core. They came in three flavors: mint, cherry and "original," which my brothers and I called barf.

Our pre-adolescent friendship ripened as we approached seventh grade. Over the summer, we choreographed dance routines to Wham! and Peter

Gabriel. The discovery that we had the same shoe size effectively doubled our footwear options—no mean objective for female tweens. We went shopping together, acquiring the requisite items for junior high attendance: Esprit bags and oversize sweaters, Ombre Rose perfume and cans of Final Net in ozone-annihilating quantities.

But it was the arrival of seventh grade that would cement our friendship. Maggie and I were locker partners and we would leave notes for each other, thick with solidarity, riddled with impressionistic punctuation. On frog dissection in Life Science: "The liver looks like a shriveled jelly bean and it's GROSS."

On teacher wardrobe in Social Studies: "Mrs. Hanson's dress = tarp with flowers. Not. Good."

On the opposite sex in PE: "Randy Warner in shorts during basketball!!! Sigh."

The notes were invariably accompanied by our signature epilogue: "Best friends 4 EVA!"

But my fondest memories of Maggie revolve around getting ready for junior high dances. Held in the local city hall, these dances were fraught with adolescent sexuality set to Michael Bolton songs. They began in the seventh grade, the year all the grade schools from the larger Spokane area runnelled together, forming a coagulant of hormones, anxiety and acid-washed jeans: a filovirus of tweendom, perfumed with Drakkar Noir and hairspray.

They required quite a bit of foreplay, these dances. The first act was procuring makeup. My mother didn't believe in makeup. Actually, it was more that makeup never really entered her mind. She was a farmer's wife with six children. Bag Balm doubled as a cow teat softener and lip gloss. Tenuous questions regarding makeup acquisition seemed out of the question. How does one ask a woman just in from delivering lambs from the barn about mascara? It seemed unfathomable.

Maggie didn't own makeup *per se*, but she had a life-sized Barbie's head, a fifth-grade birthday present bequeathed by a well-meaning aunt. You could brush and braid Barbie's hair and choose from three different makeup options—royal blue eyeshadow, candy apple red lipstick and bubblegum pink blusher—to lacquer across the plastic face. We adapted these to our purpose with gusto, skillfully blending Vaseline and Barbie makeup to desirable effect.

After applying makeup in the bedroom, Maggie and I would gather in her bathroom, faces lit by a row of 40-watt bulbs, a curling iron plugged into each side of the counter. The wallpaper was white with a tracery of yellow velvet diamonds. They marched across the walls in the dim bathroom light, the color of egg yolks and anticipation.

After an hour or so, a quorum of curls would have formed. The forehead took the longest: the far left hairs straight up, cascading down until the right just brushed the eye. The result was a battlement of bangs, a 45-degree ramp of curls—cemented in place with hair spray—that could withstand weather, tight turtlenecks and importune cheeks during slow dances.

This ritual of preening was meticulous, back-breaking work made easy with prattle. Maggie and I discussed prospective dance outfits (who would wear the coveted *Mariposa* sweater?), lamented classes and endlessly dissected the local boy population. Would Robby Newton be there? Was the rumor that he was "going out" with Carrie Hathwood true? He hadn't sat with her at lunch on Wednesday. That was a good sign, wasn't it?

This local boy population fragmented into three tiers at the dances: *anyones* (those with whom anyone could dance but shouldn't), *reliables* (those with whom most people could dance and would) and *impossibles* (those who were so popular that only an equally popular person could dance with them). Thanks to Maggie's friendship and our relative good looks, Maggie and I were squarely in the second set. This meant we could receive invitations to dance from anyone, but could only accept those from the second or first tier. Unfortunately, it also limited our ability to ask for dances—we could only approach second-tier boys. It was an endless pantomime of social maneuvering, delicate as an inoculation.

By the first junior high dance, nearly three months into school, the popularity hierarchy had already been set. At that juncture, one's social status was more firmly established than the crease ironed into our zipper-backed Guess jeans.

The exception was Randolph. At first glance, one could be forgiven for assuming Randolph was a third-tier denizen. He was slight of frame and short, two qualities less than distinguishing in a farm town with its predictable emphasis on sports. Neither was he particularly smart or clever. This ruled out familiar archetypes of nerd and class clown. Further complicating his pigeonholing was the fact that Randolph was dapper. Suspiciously so. Whereas we went to The Bon Marché and J.C. Penney to shop, Randolph wore Gap and Nordstrom's. His waffle-weave ties weren't ironic. His red leather Michael Jackson rip-off jacket actually looked sort of cool. His penny loafers were genuine leather and sported nickels.

Randolph, you see, was wealthy. To be more precise, Randolph's father was wealthy. In a town full of wheat farmers, electricians and plumbers, Randolph's father flew commercial airplanes. His house had three stories, a pool and, most luxuriously, staff. Someone came and, unthinkably, cleaned their house. This was a town where Zips was the local burger joint and McDonald's wouldn't open its doors until my senior year in high school. Where wrestling was bigger than football and kids arrived at school having already put in early-morning hours feeding cows, delivering stock and plowing. I carried my school shoes in my red Esprit bag to don after forking chicken feed covered in BBQ sauce to our pig, Dolly. In the winter months, Dolly learned to eat quickly before the BBQ sauce froze. These kinds of families don't have a cleaning lady.

Perhaps because of his money, his wardrobe or his general *savoir faire*, Randolph was outside the social hierarchy. Or perhaps it was just that his place within it was ambiguous. That is, until the party. Two weeks before the conclusion of seventh grade, Randolph issued invitations to everyone in the first and second popularity tiers. Everyone, that is, except Maggie and me.

I found out in gym class. Shandy Tomlinson, a particularly loathsome individual with blonde hair and a penchant for gum-cracking, asked if I was going to Randolph's party.

"What party?" I asked, donning the tight, kelly green pants that constituted the bottom half of our gym uniform. Seventies remnants were cruel.

"The party everyone's going to." Chew, chew, chew.

"Well not me," I replied.

"Clearly not." This was from Petra Minden, Shandy's closest friend. Giggle, smack went Shandy and her gum, a backdrop of derision.

In the sixth grade, before the shaming, I had been more popular than Petra. I recalled holding hands at recess with the third-hottest boy in elementary school while she played four square with a gaggle of social outcasts. They took turns dispiritedly bouncing the ball, their eyes on the soccer game. Thus was her condescension particularly galling.

I didn't respond to Petra, hiding the prick of tears first in my locker, then under the physical exertion of seventh-grade gym class. Never had I served the volleyball with such vim.

That afternoon while waiting for the bus, Maggie and I had the last genuine conversation we would ever have. The first had been when she'd invited me to swing. The setting for this last one was, again, outside in a schoolyard. It was March and the rain fell hard. The grassy lawn in front of the school wasn't yet established, and the concrete entryway cut a swath through a vast tract of mucky dirt. Maggie and I and countless others clustered under the overhang near the vestibule of the junior high, avoiding the water and mud while waiting for the buses to arrive.

"Did you hear about Randolph's party?" she asked, a patina of concern covering her features more effectively than any Barbie makeup. I was ready for this question. During gym class, I had already chosen anger at the clique and was ready to close ranks against them with Maggie, primed to form an all-female version of Chaplin's The Tramp and The Gamin.

"Who cares?" I responded. "I don't want to go to any party with Shandy Tomlinson anyway. Gum-smacking cow."

"But why weren't we invited?" Maggie persisted. The tears in her eyes struck my own core of self-doubt, invoking a reply more bitter than I would have initially chosen.

"I don't want to be invited. I don't want to associate with those people. Let's have our own party. We can order pizza."

This was a brash claim, as my parents had never allowed me to order pizza in my life. One, because Rosa's Pizza didn't deliver the 30 miles out of town where we lived. And two, because delivery pizza was an extravagance reserved for never. Our pizzas were Western Family generic frozen pizza with flecks of pepperoni too small to reliably identify as meat. You took the box's word for it. That I invoked pizza spoke to the desperation of the situation.

That day, that moment in the rain, was an exchange of truth. Two souls caught in an epidemic, eddying out for a moment from the contagion of popularity. Scrape away the dressing and we were crying out to each other.

I want more than our friendship, said Maggie.

Aren't I enough? I pleaded in return. It was an invitation for our friendship to be sustaining, to be sufficient.

We looked at each other for a long moment until Maggie broke the silence.

"I'm going home," she said, and began walking to where her father's car idled at the curb.

"What about the pizza?" I called after her. But Maggie gave no notice that she had heard and got into the car and rode away. I waited for the bus as her footprints slowly disappeared in the mud, erased by the rain.

Randolph's first party would prove to be our Waterloo. In the summer before eighth grade, in the aftermath of our great social failure, I would become someone who tried very hard not to care about popularity; Maggie, on the other hand, would become an anorexic.

As the summer progressed, I saw Maggie less and less. Each time, her weight slowly whittled away. A month before eighth grade began, Maggie was hospitalized. I visited her, careful not to jostle the feeding tube surgically implanted in her stomach. I stared across the bed at my best friend, cheekbones impossibly tight in her wan face, and realized that we were strangers.

I wonder, now, how much not being invited to Randolph's party played into Maggie's illness. Perhaps it didn't affect me as much because I had already been a social outcast. Perhaps those hours in the sixth grade at recess reading *Charlotte's Web* and *Anne of Green Gables* against the wall had fortified me in ways I didn't know.

What I did know, holding her hand, brittle as a twig in winter, was that I wasn't able to save Maggie as she had been able to save me.

Now, nearly 30 years later, Maggie is married but has no kids. I know this because her mother talks to mine occasionally. Small towns. From these scattershot reports, I know that she was hospitalized at various times throughout college and beyond for anorexia, which didn't stabilize until she was in her 30s. But there are lingering effects. Her organs were damaged from protracted years of illness, and would affect her ability to have children.

I'm 40 now, married and with a daughter. I haven't spoken to Maggie since we graduated from high school, although she's friends with friends on Facebook. I survey that time of my life, that time of Esprit bags and first boyfriends and Swatches, and I wonder about those hours spent in the Final Net-drenched bathroom at Maggie's house. I think on the happiness of being lent the *Mariposa* sweater and of having something equally nice—white leather moccasins with fringe—to offer in response. I recall Maggie and me frantically completing geometry sets during lunch. She would do the first 10 problems and I'd do the last 10, then we'd switch papers to copy each other's work, inserting a few mistakes so cheating wasn't suspected. I recall our locker notes of encouragement and solidarity. All of that was a kind of love, wasn't it?

But Maggie was 13, and being popular was the most important thing in the world. Sometimes the love you give someone isn't the love they want, though it might be the love they need. And all the pizza in the world won't change that.

༄

 **Jodi Teti** *is an L.A.-based writer, marketing director and churro aficionado. She graduated from Stanford University with a major in English Literature, a mistake compounded by an M.A. in 18th Century Literature from the University of Virginia. She enjoys hiking, science fiction and election years that eschew discussions of global climate change.*

BUT WOULD YOU FIGHT WITH ME FOREVER?

Lisa L. Kirchner

MY DAD WAS THE ONLY DAD I KNEW who changed jobs with a near-annual frequency. Already we'd moved from eastern Pennsylvania to Michigan to Alabama to western Pennsylvania, where we now lived in a small town outside Pittsburgh. "We're living in a suburb," my emphatically urban mother despaired, "that has no sidewalks." Throughout all this upheaval, Dad remained an unflagging optimist. He'd backed losers Gerald Ford over Jimmy Carter, and then Bobby Riggs over Billy Jean King in the tennis "Battle of the Sexes." But when Dad lined us—my mother, sister and me—up on the green-striped woolen couch in our Murrysville living room to announce his latest move, we all thought he was nuts. He was ditching his corporate job to follow his bliss. This time, we weren't going anywhere. My sister and I were a scant few years from college, and he'd bought…a *gym*?

Dad may have run so hard his toenails turned black and fell off, but to the rest of us, working out was a foreign concept. The fitness frenzy of the 1980s notwithstanding, there *were* people who didn't don sweatbands. The people in my family. My mother would prop her elbows on the gym's glass countertop over high-priced racquetball racquets and gloves, point at me with her cigarette and proclaim, "Your father knew I didn't like to exercise when he met me." Then she'd take a deep drag.

Given their differences, my parents fought. They always had, whether it was over moving or money or me and my sister I'm not sure, because they did it behind closed doors. When we were kids we'd try and listen, but we always grew bored before they did. In high school, I'd just turn up the volume on my stereo. But Mom was Catholic and dad's parents had divorced back in the 1930s. Neither of them was going to budge.

I was a sophomore at Ohio State, moving into my sixth dorm before it occurred to me I might have a problem with staying in one place—whether it be a location or a person—and that this pattern might be problematic. It didn't hit me then that part of this problem might have been that I was unwilling to fight. That's when I met Jeffrey.

Jeffrey and I were not a natural match. For one thing, we met at a drug and alcohol rehab where I was a patient and he was a volunteer. I was in college, Jeffrey hadn't gone. He worked for the city's water department, I worked at a store called Magnolia Thunderpussy Records & Tapes. Jeffrey listened to Robert Palmer without irony. He wore snakeskin boots and bolo ties, my hair was pink and my wardrobe secondhand. But Jeffrey, despite the fact that he didn't smoke, brought me cigarettes. Cartons, not packs. And for the next five years, every day, he taught me what it meant to stay.

The first time we fought, I thought we were over. This was the essence of what moving taught me about dealing with people. We were either on and we were friends, I thought, or we were off and would never speak again. Clearly now, Jeffrey and I were off. Except he didn't leave. He explained that no, he'd not noticed the birthday cards in my dorm room. That he wasn't a mind reader. That I should tell him about things that mattered. Out loud.

The very idea blew my mind. To me, fighting meant saying shitty things behind your partner's back, but with Jeff we went at it face to face. He was nothing if not reassuring. "Keesha," he'd say, because that's what he called me. "Love is not a destination. We're not getting somewhere, we're getting along. Don't worry." But I was pretty bad at not worrying.

Once driving down to Florida, we were having a quarrel that devolved into a cursing match. There was no content anymore, just a roar of expletives until we broke down laughing. From that point forward, a meekly intoned string of swear words could dispel most tensions. Having Jeffrey know my ugliest parts—my anger, my hypocrisy, the parts that I myself don't even like—and love me anyway changed me. Life became lighter. The world was not a spigot with two settings, the world was an ocean.

On what would be our last night together, we started arguing over something well-worn. Something I cannot recall. Something so trivial even we had no steam for it. We decided it was better to curl into one another, to battle it out another time.

He called the next afternoon to see if I wanted to join him at his mother's swimming pool. He'd recently left his job with the city and become a full-time scuba instructor. He often spent time in the pool practicing breathing exercises. I declined. The Columbus Museum of Art needed my services.

The next call I got was from his sister's boyfriend. Jeffrey had drowned in the pool. I stayed up all night with my friend Karen, who left her babies with her husband to sit with me while I smoked and fretted. In the morning, I didn't know what to do but go to work, wearing my black linen suit. My boss looked at me and laughed, "Did somebody die?" I went home for the day, or possibly the next few days. At times, I wondered if our postponed fight had unconsciously caused the accident, if it had made Jeffrey lose focus in that split-second between life and death. I dreamed of Jeff while asleep and awake, and the difference between the two times is blurred. Much later, when I saw a picture of myself taken that summer while I was supposedly at work, I looked just like that, as if I were sleepwalking—no makeup, hair and clothes askew and a vacant look in my eyes. I was 24 and knew no one would ever love me like that again.

To some extent, no one ever *has* loved me like that again. Not that this has played out in the way I imagined then. No two loves are alike. Not if you're trying. When I did meet and marry another man some 10 years later, another Geoffrey even, the relationships were entirely different. Geoff had gone to private schools. He had impeccable taste in music and books and all things arty. And we did not fight. Never. Clearly this was a new and improved version of me in a new and improved version of love; I thought I had kicked my demons.

When one day my husband, a journalist, called from Baghdad, he was letting me know he'd not been killed by that day's huge bomb. "The world's news is happening here," he panted. "I wish we could live here."

Most people would've murmured politely and changed the subject. Not I. To me, once a desire to relocate was announced, I was as good as gone. As it so happened, a client of mine had recently announced they'd be opening a branch in the Persian Gulf. "What would you say to Qatar?" was how I replied to Geoffrey. Soon we were off. This was meant to be.

Except it wasn't. Moving overseas strained our relationship. I'd taken a regular job after more than five years running my own consulting business, and now Geoffrey was freelancing. Except that he didn't pick up assignments. When he finally broke down and took a low-level job, I was devastated. I wanted so badly to yell, "I've given up everything to create a life for you that I'd kill to have!" Instead, as we drove to his new job that first morning, I said, "You don't have to take this job if you don't want to, you know." He replied, "I know." And that was that. Or so I thought, but of course, in much the same way my parents' distress was obvious, the tension was a presence.

We gave it a year, but finally Geoffrey returned to the States to look for work. A few weeks after that, he called to tell me he wanted a divorce. Perhaps because it was so immediate, Geoffrey's disappearance from my life felt no less shocking than Jeffrey's death, and no less final. He simply said, "I want a divorce." When I told him I did not, he said, "This is not negotiable." We did not linger on the phone, or ever again.

For a time, I moved into my still-married parents' basement. While there, I found myself desperate to get my hands on their wedding pictures. Growing up, I'd pored over these black-and-whites, wondering where they'd gone wrong. They were so stunning—my mother, chin tucked, adjusting her veil. My father, resting his hand on Mom's impossibly small waist. Both dashing through a sea of rice. Now I wanted to know what they'd done right.

"For crying out loud!" I heard my dad yell at my mom in frustration, anxious at her dawdling when he wanted to get to the gym he still runs. I cringed, still hating their fights. It would be another eight years before my parents would celebrate their 50th birthdays, but only one before I'd witness my father become an anxious caretaker of my mother, recording her blood pressure daily, using his knowledge of health and fitness to craft a special cancer-fighting diet and even learning how to cook. Even so, not knowing what was to come, it struck me that this might be what they'd done right after all. Maybe if you won't fight *with* your partner, you won't fight *for* your partner. Or maybe that was too easy, too spigot-like. The wonder of love is its god-like unknowability. Just when I think I've got it sorted out, love kicks my ass again. Jeffrey used to tell me, "I'd rather be the steamship than the tugboat. The steamship doesn't get ruffled by life's waves." It occurred to me now that the steamship also kept moving.

When I finally did find those wedding images, something came into sharp focus, something I'd never noticed. The photos had always been in a stack; I'd always attributed the lack of an album to a lack of time. Now I saw, written in the upper right corner of each photo, the word "proof." My parents never bothered to get prints.

❦

**Lisa L. Kirchner** *is the author of* Hello American Lady Creature: What I Learned as a Woman in Qatar. *At one time she was simultaneously the dating columnist for an alternative newsweekly, bridal editor for a society rag and the religion reporter for a gay and lesbian newspaper. She lives in New York City. She writes and teaches yoga pretty much everywhere she goes. More at www.LisaLKirchner.com.*

SO WHAT IS UNCONDITIONAL LOVE ANYWAY?

Bari Benjamin

BEFORE I TRAVELED TO MOSCOW 16 years ago to adopt my two-year-old brown-eyed baby girl, I fantasized what she and *we* would be like together. I imagined she would be cuddly, sweet and feminine, wearing frilly dresses and brightly colored barrettes in her carefully brushed hair. I dreamed how I would hold her in my arms at bedtime, rock her to sleep and softly sing lullabies until her eyes gently closed. I pictured her running to me when frightened, and I would swoop her up, crooning "sha, sha" in her ear, until her heartbeat slowed and she was calm.

Because I am a clinical social worker and had practiced psychotherapy for 15 years, I felt confident I could handle any difficulties that could arise. No, I didn't work with children, but I had researched possible problems that institutionalized children endure. I had read about children with Reactive Attachment Disorder. In its most severe form, these are the children who torture animals and have no empathy. I believed this was rare (my own denial perhaps), although I did anticipate anger issues and developmental delays. After all, my soon-to-be little girl had lived in an orphanage (they call them "baby homes" in Moscow) for over a year. There were bound to be repercussions from not having a mommy to bond with.

Since I embarked upon this journey as a single mom with no biological family nearby, I structured a Pittsburgh family for her. My two closest friends, male and female, committed to be her aunt and uncle. Not knowing whether I would ever marry again, I recognized the importance of a male role model in her life. I thought I had covered my bases. I thought I was prepared. The truth is, I wasn't.

For the first year or two, Liliya was more prickly than cuddly. When I held out my arms for her, she looked away, or she sat in a corner on the floor by herself. Following the advice of child psychologists, I alone fed, bathed and rocked her to sleep for a solid year. But she frequently ignored me. One morning at Starbucks, I turned my back ever so briefly to put cream in my coffee. When I turned around, she was sitting with a family of four, smiling. I quickly whisked her away, and she stiffened in my arms, her smile replaced by a scowl.

My fantasy of my girly girl was just that. A fantasy. She refused pretty dresses and threw them on the floor. (To this day, she prefers jeans and hoodies to dresses and heels.) When scared (the noise of the vacuum cleaner frightened her), she resisted my touch and curled up on the floor, sobbing. Car rides punctuated with blood-curdling screams from the back seat started my day. She was inconsolable.

Although these behaviors softened as time progressed, those early years challenged my patience and my self-image as a parent and a mom. My ability to soothe and comfort her waned thin during her frequent tantrums. Memories of yelling at her to stop still haunt me and make me cringe.

Once, she told her fourth-grade teacher that the eczema on her arm was really rope burns that I had given her. How alarmed I was by her lying. Then there was the time I noticed her clutching something in her jacket pocket as we exited the CVS store. "What do you have, Liliya?"

"Nothing, Mommy."

"No, let me see, please."

She uncurled her fist. A shiny keychain appeared. What to do? I sat in my car, silent. Thinking. I could return the keychain myself. That way, I would avoid shaming her. I had learned that shame is a predominant emotion for some children who suffer from early trauma. They carry it with them in the pit of their souls and react angrily when it surfaces. But what would she learn?

"We need to give this back. We'll do it together. I'll hold your hand."

When the store manager gently explained that shoplifting is a crime and that the police could be called, I watched my daughter's cheeks flame red. She ran out of the store and refused to climb in the car. After an hour of coaxing and reassuring her that everyone makes mistakes, and that I still loved her, we started back home.

When I recall those years, though, they seem trivial compared to what came next.

It got bad. Really bad. Adolescence exploded at 15, a firecracker that wouldn't die. Layers of emotional issues stacked against each other like rungs on a teetering ladder, ready to collapse at any minute. There were the usual separation-individuation issues a teenage daughter needs to negotiate to distinguish herself from her mother. The drive to be different, the impulse to push away, the eye-rolling when I spoke, the one-word responses to my questions, the *leave me alone* one minute and *cuddle with me, Mama* the next. I get that. *That's* normal.

But the rage—her rage was relentless. At any moment and often for no apparent reason, she spewed venom and hateful feelings about me, about her life and, sadly, about herself. "I hate you, you bitch," she screamed, running out the door, coatless, one frigid winter night after I had confiscated her phone for breaking a house rule. I found her shivering in our neighborhood gazebo. She collapsed in my arms, sobbing, "I'm worthless. Why did she give me up? Why?" I held her hard and soothed her long. But the curse words written later that evening, in black magic markers on the freshly painted walls of her bedroom, were the foreshadowing of more horror to come.

One morning as she dressed for school, I spied something on her arm. *Oh my God,* I thought. *What is that?* Up and down, up and down, an intricate pattern of zigzag cuts with blood crusted on the edges. She couldn't meet my eyes. We rushed to the nearby medical facility in case she needed stitches to avoid scarring. I prayed this was a one-time occurrence, but it wasn't. Two hellish years followed, with more cutting and running away for several days at a time.

"Where are you?" I texted, the first time she left. She was 14 years old.

"None of your business."

"You need to come home." Silence.

Another time she agreed to meet me at a coffee shop. Relief flooded through me when we drove home and she grabbed something to eat in the kitchen. I calmly persuaded her to stay home, go back to school, start over. But then, she walked toward the door.

"Wait. What are you doing?"

"I'm leaving with my friends."

"Listen, if you do this again, I'll have to call the police," I said as I followed her out the door.

"Fuck you. I don't care. Go ahead."

The police, by the way, were not helpful.

On-the-street alcohol? Drugs? Sex? I worried about the trouble she could get into. We tried individual therapy. We tried family therapy. Nothing changed. I realized I couldn't keep her safe.

I agonized. I knew given her history of abandonment, sending her away seemed unthinkable. How could I repeat the original trauma? And yet, how could I keep her safe at home? The voices in my head argued. Sometimes they yelled at each other. There was Mama Bari, and there was seasoned-psychotherapist Bari.

Psychotherapist Bari: *You can't send her away. How would she feel? She'll hate you forever.*

Mama Bari: *But what am I supposed to do? Sit back and watch something awful happen to her?*

When I researched the residential facility for adopted teens that focused on attachment and bonding with their parents, a slow stream of hope trickled through me. The facility's treatment philosophy included an adopt-a-dog program. They believed that students gained insight and empathy by working toward becoming adoptive moms themselves. This empathy would then theoretically transfer to their parental relationships. By raising the golden retriever puppies, the students experienced love, attachment and responsibility. If they fulfilled all the requirements, they participated in an adoption ceremony and became moms, able to leave with their dogs when ready. *This was it!* I thought. Even though we already lived with an elderly cat, Liliya had always wanted a dog. My gut told me that if I didn't try everything possible, I would regret it someday.

On her first day in the program, I watched my daughter gently hold the tiny puppy that would become hers. As she stroked his dark red coat, my eyes teared as I glimpsed the tenderness buried inside her. I left that evening with mixed feelings of relief, hope and sadness swirling inside me. My life had been structured around caring for this girl. Now a staff of therapists was caring for her. For days afterward, I felt lost, floating, not grounded. Yes, I had my work and Liliya's Pittsburgh-made family for support. But I didn't have her; the wondering and worrying ceased. No more: *What will she be like today? Will she take off today?* I struggled to fill that hole.

The program was hard work for everyone: monthly visits for family therapy and retreats, weekly Skyping therapy, frequent phone calls with Liliya during which she expressed her hurts and angry feelings. Initial phone conversations went like this:

Liliya: "I don't want to talk to you."

Me: "Okay. Just wanted to know if you're okay."

Click.

And sometimes she just refused my calls.

Our conversations affected me. If she shared her thoughts and feelings, my mood soared. If she was angry and withdrawn, my mood sank. It was an emotional rollercoaster, and I needed to find a way to get off.

The first time I visited her, she refused to see me. Resentment bubbled up inside me, as it had been a plane ride and a lengthy drive to reach her. After talking to her therapist, she relented, but the visit was short. Many times, she couldn't say goodbye and abruptly pushed me away. Therapy sessions were tough, intense. I bore the brunt of so much anger. Sometimes I just wanted to yell, "I'm *not* the mother who left you in a train station. That wasn't me."

After months of listening to her angry, hurt feelings, I learned the importance of validating her emotions, even if I didn't understand them. I had to express my feelings in matter-of-fact tones, for Liliya experienced even a slightly raised voice as anger. Learning a new way of communicating with her was like learning a foreign language. But we persevered together, and I sensed a gradual shift: more warmth than anger, more affection, even a bit of gratefulness. Could this have been a result of her raising and training the puppy she called Albert Einstein?

During this time, the Reuters Investigative Reports, aired on NBC, exposed a website where adoptive parents of troubled teens could give their children away to other families, often to virtual strangers. Inga, from Russia, adopted at the age of 12, was given away within a year. After a few months, she was given away to another family, then yet again. They called it "re-homing." In my darkest moments, I wondered if I had done a gentler version of re-homing. Then I would remind myself that she is safe, *she is safe.*

Friends often wondered how I had survived the turmoil. They knew of parents who had relinquished their parental rights to the court system. A part of me understood the fear and helplessness of these parents, but just like re-homing, I found relinquishing my rights unimaginable.

My daughter is back home now. Is she better? Yes—less angry, less self-destructive. That's better. Do I see the reflection of the values I've tried to teach her? Not really. My daughter rarely glances at a book, and working out to her is like going to the dentist. And we couldn't be more opposite. I enjoy meeting friends outside of our home. She's content sitting in her room and texting. I realize we only had the nurture piece and not the nature one, but I had hoped for more similarities.

I've often wondered about the saying, "Only a mother will love unconditionally." Did my mother love me unconditionally? I felt loved, but what if I had resisted her expectations of me? Would I have only felt her disapproval? I remember knowing from a very early age that college was in my future. I joke that she talked about college as I started kindergarten. There was no debating it; it was mandatory. If I had refused more education, would her love have wavered?

My journey continues with my daughter. I've had to let go of my wishes and expectations for her life. She is in control now. I'm not. It has been, and is still, a gut-wrenching, agonizing process. I have to just plain love her for who she is and whoever she may become. Oddly enough, rather than my heart constricting, it has ballooned, made larger by this commitment. And I deeply cherish the loving moments of closeness, however fleeting they are.

Just this morning, while driving my daughter to school, I glanced over at her, and my heart swelled with love. She was singing and rocking to the music on the radio, a smile on her face. She looked happy. I thought of the journey behind us and the journey ahead. My eyes filled with tears at the intensity of my emotions. I told her this and instead of pushing me away with sarcasm or, worse, indifference, she touched my tears and softly whispered, "It's okay, Mama. It's okay."

 **Bari Benjamin** *is a former English teacher turned psychotherapist. She lives and practices psychotherapy in Pittsburgh. Bari has written stories since she was a young girl and vividly remembers her first rejection from a children's magazine. Since then, she has had many more but has also published personal essays in magazines and anthologies. When not dancing enthusiastically in Zumba class, you might see her walking arm in arm with her daughter and her daughter's seriously smart golden retriever named Albert Einstein.*

PATRICIA

Richard Zielinski

WHEN I WAS 16 AND LIVING in the Bloomfield neighborhood of Pittsburgh, my best friend Norm asked me if I wanted to go to his uncle's house in Lawrenceville to drop off some tools that his father had borrowed. He didn't tell me he had a 13-year-old cousin, Patricia. Norm knew I was obsessed with another girl, Linda, and I guess he was trying to break the spell she had put on me.

When we got to Norm's uncle's, the sun was beating down and the wind barely whispered. Patricia was sitting on the concrete porch steps with her girlfriend. She was shaded by a green and white awning and surrounded by a white metal railing with poles that looked like twisted licorice sticks. As we approached, Patricia frowned, but I didn't know if it was for me or for Norm. She had a cute mouth with lips as thin and pink as rose petals. She was a doll. When our eyes met, there was instant attraction.

Of course, I had to impress her, so I took out a rubber ball and played a game of three flies with Norm. I jumped, stretched and wiggled. The sun scorched the asphalt street. My tennis shoes squeaked with every move. Patricia's frown turned into a smirk. She laughed whenever I banged into the parked cars or had to run frantically down the street to grab the ball before it disappeared down the sewer hole.

Then I tried the suave approach.

"Hi," I said.

Over the last two years, before I met Patricia, Linda had kept me on her leash. It wasn't hard to do. Two years before that, my parents had driven me to Hollidaysburg to become a priest at a Franciscan seminary. I studied Latin and prayed feverishly. Then one day my parents brought up a visitor, a girl I had always had a crush on. Shortly after that visit, I left the seminary. I had become mesmerized by the other sex. I fell in love with all of them, but I struck out with all of them, too.

My buddies and I used to gather on the steps of a corner grocery store at the bottom of Taylor Street. We were Bill's best customers, so he never bothered us or chased us away.

Linda lived a few houses up the street, and I would see her sitting on her front steps wearing short shorts. We both lived on the same street, so we knew each other.

But we never really talked to each other. I hadn't seen her in the two years I was away but, man, she had developed into a teenage tigress. She had short black hair, an aquiline nose, luscious lips and lovely legs. It was lust at first sight. She called me Richie. It sounded so personal because no one but my mother had ever called me that.

One day, for some odd reason, I walked up and stood next to her. I kept licking my lips. I wanted to kiss her. We talked, but it was just gibberish. Her brown eyes devoured me and she ran her hand up my arm. It was the first time we had ever touched each other. We both suddenly surrendered to a sweet succulent kiss that seemed to last a lifetime. I was completely gone. From that moment on, she owned me.

But Linda kept my panting under control by sharing herself with other guys. She let my hands wander anywhere they wanted to, but then the next day she would be strolling down Taylor Street, holding hands with some wavy-haired Italian as I sat fuming on the glider behind the wooden railing of my porch.

When I saw Patricia's young vibrant innocence that summer day, I experienced a pleasant reprieve from the hot, steamy affair with Linda. I began to realize that sweetness and romance were once again possible.

But then Norm yelled that it was time to leave. I looked at Patricia.

"Will I see you again?" Patricia asked. Her eyes sparkled and a smile softened her face.

My heart stuttered more than my mouth when I said, "Tomorrow?"

She shook her bouncy blond hair up and down, and I waved goodbye as Norm dragged me by the shirttail up Fisk Street and back to earth.

The next evening, I walked up Taylor Street and down Idaline Way. I made a right, past the Bloomfield Pool and the parked cars and the occasional dual-purposed chairs silently proclaiming "This is my spot." Linda was sitting on a high porch with her girlfriend, taunting me.

"Going to see your girlfriend, Richie?" There were no secrets in a small town like Bloomfield.

I just shook my head and gave her a nonchalant wave. I walked faster, trying to break the puppet strings still attaching me to Linda, but they just stretched like over-tuned guitar strings. I crossed a busy intersection. Horns blared and angry words burst from open driver-side windows. As I hurried down Fisk Street, I could see Patricia on the steps. She didn't wave. She smiled, and her eyes met mine. I reached out my hand and she took it, and then we held each other. There were no words, but I could feel her warm breath on my neck. I will never forget how close to heaven I felt in that moment. I could hear some of those puppet strings go *ping*, and I hoped that someday I would say, "Who's Linda?"

In the evenings, Patricia and I would sit side by side in the small dark vestibule inside her storm door. It was our little corner of the world. We'd whisper enticing endearments and explore each other's lips. We'd run our hands all over each other, discovering the muscles and the softness, the fragrance and the scents. Her long legs lay in my lap while my hand caressed her face. I kissed her languorous eyes, and my hand slipped past the nipples of her tiny breasts. I felt her slim thighs and moved up to a warm, moist mound of silken fur.

"Do you like that?" she asked.

I smiled and kissed her deeply.

The next two years brought us closer. We went to movies, sipped sodas on drugstore stools. We swiveled and looked at each other with puckered mouths. At the Bloomfield Pool, we splashed and dunked each other. I took her to high-school dances where we gazed into each other's eyes to the soothing sound of Scott English singing "High on a Hill." We talked for hours on the phone. Sometimes she would fall asleep, and I would have to whisper loudly to tell her to hang up.

How could it not last?

For Christmas, I gave Patricia a silver bracelet with my name engraved on it, but she wanted something more permanent. She pulled out a silver-coated comb, and her face grew somber and her eyes penetrated mine.

"Cut me."

I heard what she said but I couldn't react. She placed the comb teeth down on her arm, put my hand over it and pushed down. Then she ran the comb sharply across her arm. Blood started oozing from the wound it left. I reached for my handkerchief to stop the bleeding, and suddenly I felt the comb slicing against my arm with the same result, and I will always carry the scar, just as she wanted me to.

Patricia was aware of Linda. She knew Linda was older and had a more physical hold on me than she did. One day, when Patricia's parents weren't home, she led me upstairs to her bedroom. She sat on the bed and started taking her clothes off. But I couldn't do it. This wasn't what I wanted from her.

"Don't you want me?" she asked.

"Not like this," I said.

"But you'd do it to her, wouldn't you?"

She flung herself off the bed and ran down the steps. I followed helplessly and stood on the landing, wondering where this was going.

She threw the front door open and glared at me. "Get out!"

"I want your love, Patricia. That means more than sex. Haven't I proved that to you?"

She wouldn't even look at me. So, I left.

After that moment, whenever I called her, she would hang up without even talking to me, except to say, "I don't want to ever see you again."

Did I send her flowers? No. Did I ask her to her junior prom? No. It should have been an easy choice: someone who loved me or someone who flicked me away like cigarette ashes. But I threw it all away. Linda begged me to take her to her senior prom, and I couldn't resist the sexual pull she had on me. I bought her a pink rose bouquet that she pinned on her white-gloved arm. Her prom dress reminded me of a lamp shade. My arms would have had to grow another foot before I could put them around her waist. We had our picture taken, and she looked like an aristocrat posing with her latest wide-eyed champion stallion. But then she spent the night flirting with other guys, while I stood by not knowing what to do with my hands and feeling like a neglected poodle. We drove home with another couple, and she wouldn't let me touch her. So many things went through my mind: the other guys, the times I had no idea where she was or who she was with. I became fed up with playing "she loves me, she loves me not." I decided that was it, and I felt a cool refreshing breeze go through my heart. I was free, free to be with Patricia.

The next day I called Patricia, but no one answered. I slammed the phone down and rushed out the door. I walked fast. I ran, then walked, then ran some more. I was sweating and out of breath when I knocked.

Patricia threw opened the door, livid as sunburn. "Did you think I wouldn't find out?"

I just stood there like a mime with swinging arms and trembling lips, and no defense.

"We're through. Do you hear me? Through!"

She slammed the door in my face.

For months, I drifted along the neighborhood in a trance. I had lost my chance at romance, and I was lonely. The seminary had been a curse. It didn't protect me from lust, and it couldn't prevent me from destroying what I thought of then as a sweet innocent love.

After that, I put all my energy into sports and joined a softball team that played under the Bloomfield Bridge on a field called Dean's. Patricia somehow found out where and when the game was. While I was playing shortstop, Patricia began to waltz past the fence of Dean's Field and flaunt her new boyfriend. Balls would hit me in the chest and bounce off my head every time she walked by.

Why didn't she walk down another street? Was she trying to make me jealous? Was she trying to give me another chance to win her love? It puzzled me and often kept me awake at night.

One day at the field, she called me over to the fence. I didn't see her boyfriend.

She said, "Walt wants to fight you because of what you did to me."

"What did I do to you?"

"He'll tell you. He'll be waiting inside the cemetery."

It sounded like a setup, so I asked Norm to come with me. When we walked into the back entrance of the cemetery that Friday night, Walt had his own bodyguard, who had to have been seven feet tall. I noticed Patricia and her girlfriend huddled together across the street. The cemetery was dark. Clouds drifted past the full moon, causing the tombstones to light up like flash bulbs. I had never seen Walt up close, so I was surprised when I recognized him as a friend from the seminary.

"Walt?"

"Is that you, Rich?"

"Why do you want to fight me?" I asked.

"She told me that you wanted to fight *me*."

Then we both looked at her and knew she just wanted us to fight over her.

Patricia began to cry, but they were tears of rage. She had thought she was getting revenge because I had asked Linda and not her to the prom, while failing to realize that Linda was history to me now. I knew that I had betrayed Patricia, but with her revenge plot, we had reached a point now where we both knew that nothing could ever get us back to that sweet love we had shared. Patricia was history to me now, too.

Walt and I shook hands, while Patricia and her girlfriend left without a backward glance.

Four years later, I graduated from college and spent a semester student-teaching in Tarentum. I turned on the news one summer night and heard that the government had cancelled all occupational deferments. It was 1970, and President Nixon pulled my number out of a fishbowl. I traded my suit for Navy whites.

While overseas on a Navy destroyer, I operated powerful radio transmitters that ruined my hearing. I also handled communications between the sailors and their loved ones. Occasionally I had to relay Dear John letters that came in the mail. Two were addressed to me. Linda told me she was married, and Patricia wrote that she was engaged to a guy named Harry. By then, I wasn't human anymore. The war and the Navy had destroyed any teaching aspirations I'd had. They had destroyed my hearing and maybe even my soul. I was bitter, and I had begun stuffing my loneliness with one-night stands that left me as empty as a dried-up stream. So it was no surprise to me that I couldn't care less what Linda did. But I did still have a shred of decency left. On leave that Christmas, I walked down in dress blues to visit Patricia and her family to apologize to her and to wish her the best on her engagement. She took me outside, and we talked about the pain we had caused each other, and how we still had feelings for one another. She kissed me hard. The snow was coming down heavily, and she was trembling. She grabbed my arms, and her eyes were pleading.

"Just say you don't want me to marry Harry and I won't."

I bit my lips and ran my tongue over them. I was tempted. I couldn't believe she still loved me, but I just couldn't do it. I couldn't ruin her new life. I felt then that I couldn't give her what Harry could give her. I could only give her more pain and betrayal. So I said, "I can't."

She pushed herself away from me. Her eyes seemed to glaze over. Her head sank to her chest. And when she looked back up, devoid of all expression, she said, "Leave. Just go. Please."

I never saw her again. And I miss her.

꙳

**Richard Zielinski** *lives in Pittsburgh, Pennsylvania, with his lovely wife Carmella and two adopted dogs, Chloe and Neuman. He is a Navy veteran and a former English teacher at Tarentum Junior High. Richard also self-published a book of short stories titled* The Short Stories of a Strange Man, *available on Amazon, in which he "used his wild and varied experiences and added much exaggeration." He is currently working on a second book of short stories, but don't hold your breath. The first one took 30 years to finish.*

THE OKAYEST BROTHER

Ellen E. Hyatt

My existence did not matter to my brother. Not a bit. That's what I thought for years. It took me over three decades to realize I could be wrong.

These days, when in my sunroom, I sometimes think back to those childhood times. I tilt the blinds on windows and invite in enough light to see again the room off the kitchen in our house at 645 Baldwin Street in Bridgeville, Pennsylvania. There, on rainy or wintry days, my brother and I, ages four and six, would play.

In the playroom, there were windows, a door leading to the back porch, a tray for shoes, hooks for coats and a cot. I never did learn why the cot was placed there, though it did end up serving a purpose: the cot became a table for my tea parties. Dolls leaned on each other to sit as straight as they possibly could on the unstable surface. Each doll would hold a cup and saucer in her lap and await my pouring of imaginary tea from a Blue Willow teapot. These dishes were part of the set I had received as a gift from my maternal grandmother. She lived in Hawaii, and the set had traveled all the way over water and land. Unbroken…to me…for me. I can hear my mother's voice: "Ellen, do you think you're old enough and will you be careful enough with these china dishes?" I shook my head and reinforced my nonverbal response with words: "Yes, I am. Yes! Yes, I will. Yes!" I felt proud to be able to care for this child-sized set of china all by myself.

During the tea party, I engaged in long conversations with the dolls. They asked me for "more tea, please." This began a whole string of words that rhymed: *bee, fee, gee, key, knee, me, see, we.* Each doll took her turn with a word until one remarked, "I thank the BEE that made the hoNEY for my TEA cooKIE." I thanked the dolls for coming and asked them to please visit with me again because my mother was sewing new dresses for them.

After each tea party for the dolls, I would place all the china back in the box the set came in, attentive to the shape of each piece, so that I could match it with the spot designed especially for it. I thought it was like putting together a jigsaw puzzle. The cardboard frames supported and protected the handles of the cups, as well as the handle and spout of the teapot. I've been told that, though I was only six and played with the china incessantly throughout the winter months, I never broke one piece. When not in use, the set rested in the box designed for it, and the box lay hidden safely under the cot.

With a similar degree of passion and attention, my brother "Baby Jim" (the appellation I'm told I gave him on the day he was born) played cowboys. He was short for his age, but he skillfully captured the cowboy swagger. In particular, he imagined he was Hopalong Cassidy, the fictional cowboy hero with a white horse named Topper who appeared on television.

When the television show was on, Baby Jim's dark eyes widened in wild excitement, and he would jump on the arm of an overstuffed chair. There, he'd ride along with Hopalong. When the program would end and Hopalong's face would be in freeze frame a while, my little brother would ritualistically run to the screen to kiss Hopalong goodbye. Then Hopalong would fade away until the next week.

In the playroom, Baby Jim and I usually played at different times. But on *that* day, we didn't.

On *that* day, my little brother wore tiny cowboy boots with a classic Old West design in brown and white. He probably also wore a holster/gun set, unless he had again left it outside by the garage where rain rusted it or, as frequently happened, some kid stole it.

On *that* day, Baby Jim brought to the playroom a rope for lassoing and trick-roping. Like a miniature Will Rogers, my brother tried changing the size of the loop and the speed of the rotation. Before the dolls or I realized what was happening, my brother had jumped on the cot. His landing upset the calm, refined atmosphere of the playroom, transforming it into a Wild West cattle drive and, simultaneously, a reenactment of the Gunfight at the O.K. Corral. Trying to throw the rope around a target (one of the doll's heads), my brother was oblivious to my screaming demands. "Stop! Stop it, you dummy! Help! Somebody, help!"

The roundup abruptly converted the cot to a bucking bronco. My dolls trembled, china collided. My make-believe world crashed to the floor.

Picking up bits of blue and white china through tears, I must have vowed revenge. I grabbed his cowboy hat and jumped on it, in hopes that it would break into pieces just as my Blue Willow dishes had. I don't remember the rest with accuracy, only that I knew Chicken Little was right: the sky had fallen. It was being swept up with a broom and dustpan and thrown in the trash.

At some point during the roundup, my brother jumped off the cot, landed on the floor, scrambled to his feet and stood there. He was speechless, motionless. Then, his tiny four-year-old face started making the twitchy movements my parents used to scold him for. Until my brother was properly diagnosed as having earaches and allergies, he was readily accused of making "bad faces" and told to stop it. These maladies caused him to blink a lot and stretch his mouth wide to ease the pressure in his ears. Those facial movements resulted in his receiving a lot of negative attention, which in turn would cause him to feel anxious. Then, even more facial twitches would involuntarily occur to start the cycle all over again. In the playroom that day, I was so upset that I hoped his face would freeze in that nervous twitchy way.

Not surprisingly, my brother's life and my life diverged. Sure, my brother continued growing up, as did I. Our interests, though, never overlapped. We even studied at the same school for a time, but he was all things *sports*. He had been a superb shortstop on his Little League team, a fast runner and a wrestler. He owned a collection of eight-by-ten Pittsburgh Pirate baseball pictures. Autographed. He could lie on the floor for hours while watching just about every sport on television.

I, on the other hand, was all things *words*. I wrote a little for the school newspaper, rewrote notes for history tests in my notebook until they looked perfect, read and reread *Wuthering Heights* from the library, and rewrote O. Henry's "The Gift of the Magi" for a play at Sunday school. I talked to friends on the phone. I kept a secret diary with a key. There, I would write about shades of lipstick my girlfriends and I were going to buy, what colors my favorite teachers wore and the blue eyes of the tall new boy in English class.

When I was away at college, my mother sent me a letter about my brother's chemistry grade being in jeopardy because of fines he owed. I understood: breakage, of course! Unlike the Blue Willow china, however, my brother was going to have to accept responsibility for paying for the beakers, crucibles and test tubes that he had broken during the lab component of his chemistry course.

Baby Jim did graduate and began working part-time for a farmer. My grown-up brother had a job delivering eggs. *That* I could *not* imagine...all that potential breakage, you know. Two people from the same family can be so different. Despite our differences, my brother began to share his earnings with me. Baby Jim sent me money from his wages to help with my college expenses. Although I appreciated his help immensely, I don't recall there ever being a letter. None of the *words* I craved. Just a short note scribbled on the lined notebook paper that he wrapped around the bills in the envelope.

When I completed college, returned to my hometown and began teaching, my brother loaned me his car to get to and from work. By that time he was working at a Pittsburgh steel mill. He took a bus to and from his job until I made enough money to buy a car for myself. Although we were living in the same town, we rarely had a conversation.

After a few years, when my brother and I lived on our own as independent adults in separate towns, I'd receive birthday cards from him with a printed verse and the light, barely visible:

Love,
bro

On the rare occasion when my brother called, the opening of his minimalistic conversation was, "Hello, what's up?" Befuddled, I'd wonder what to say because it was *he* who had called *me*. I'd think to myself: shouldn't he be the one to have something to say? Instead he said just those three words. Well, four, because he would say "hello" as two words, "hel" then "lo."

For me, only *words* translated to love. I always longed for more in response to my notes and letters. I needed my brother's *words* to deliver details of his life, *words* to express how he was feeling, *words* to summarize a dialogue between him and his friends, *words* to hear questions about my life, *words* to explain his aspirations and *words* to plan for us to see each other.

But my brother did not make or communicate plans. With a faint smile and a remnant of that cowboy swagger, he would merely, occasionally, show up at my door because he would be on his way to some friend's home in the area. He'd sit on my sofa in silence, watch television for a while, then announce, "Well, gotta get goin'." And he'd give what has come to be known as his characteristic hug, one of the firmest and warmest hugs ever known. Then, poof! He'd be gone without a word. I used to think that maybe that hug could hang in the air as a reminder: *Yes, Ellen, your brother actually was here.* Here is his hug, rather like the iconic smile of the Cheshire Cat in Lewis Carroll's *Alice's Adventures in Wonderland*.

A few months ago, I was in an antique shop and saw a collection of pieces from a child's Blue Willow china set. I thought about buying the remnants but didn't. A couple of days later, I went back to look for them but, of course, they were gone. Seeing the dishes made me recall the incident *that* day in the playroom. And…I began having a different interpretation of it. I think maybe my brother wanted me for a playmate that day. Maybe, even at four and six, we could have reached some sort of compromise that would have blended dolls and cowboys, china and lariats. I don't know. Maybe we just needed to be nicer to each other just a little bit more.

I have come to acknowledge that my brother's nonverbal gestures were indeed messages of love. He demonstrated love through his actions, often doing something nice for others. So, for a long time, I did not—could not—recognize these wordless messages from my brother.

My brother stays in touch more often now, due to the convenience that email and texting avail. And, just recently, he even called to say the words "Happy Birthday" because he would be mailing my birthday card late. It was the first time we had *heard* each other's words in more than two years.

Just as I learned long ago that the petals of a daisy do not determine whether one person really loves another, I have also learned that words are not the only means of showing love. As a matter of fact, many times after a long, wordy email message from me, my brother's response is the text abbreviation "k." And, these days, that has come to be more than "k" with me.

**Ellen E. Hyatt** *welcomes occasions to connect with Pittsburgh, her hometown. There, Ellen became a Fellow of the Western Pennsylvania Writing Project, which encourages educators to write and value writing as a process. Ellen says putting words to paper for "The Okayest Brother" was a joy and a reminder that publishing opportunities are also a delightful part of the writing process. Though living in Summerville, South Carolina, the birthplace of sweet tea, Ellen avoids hosting tea parties for dolls. After the "Blue Willow incident," she's even refused registering for a china pattern. Recently, her husband surprised her with some miniature dishes: vintage Blue Willow. She's vowed to keep them away from cots and cowboys.*

384 DAYS

Megan Arnold

I don't remember exactly how the infatuation started. Before Cal caught my eye, my diary entries were filled with accounts of spending time with my friends, what I did that day and venting my feelings. Then, right around my 16th birthday, I began to see Cal in a different light.

> *12/04/07 Tuesday 11:06 p.m. My Birthday!!*
>
> *So today I turned 16! Woo! No one put anything on my locker, but that's cool. My computer animation class sang to me (it was just Cal and Mr. Stone), but it's the thought that counts!*

I was 16 with braces and unmanageable curly hair. And I was an adorable height so that when you hugged me, you could pick me up. I feared getting into trouble and followed the rules to the letter. Cal had dark hair and gorgeous blue eyes. He was a class clown, but I was enamored by his sense of humor. He used to wear a thin, black hair tie around his forearm, and—more importantly—he was older than me.

My high school friends gently reminded me that Cal was out of my league. I, however, did not let that dissuade me from gushing over him. I would actively search for him in the hallways between classes and during lunch. It wasn't because I wanted to talk to him or get his attention. It was because I wanted to see him. Being a senior, he was graduating that year. That meant I only had a small window of time to get him to like me back. I had never been on a date, had my first kiss or held hands. Yet none of these small details persuaded me that Cal was a lost cause. I was going to show him that we were perfect for each other.

My first plan of action was to discover what he liked and start to like it as well. Fake it till you make it. Music was the easiest route. These were the days of AIM and MySpace. You could discover the precious nuggets of information about a person through their profiles. Cal was into the band Nine Inch Nails (NIN, for short). It was a good enough place to start. I spent my evenings in front of the computer looking up their songs on YouTube and then downloading the ones I liked from LimeWire. Now I had a perfect conversation starter. I began dropping hints because that's what ladies do. I included a NIN reference in one of my projects in the class we shared. Okay, I admit that hint was pretty heavy-handed. But it worked. He spoke to me during a lull in the class period.

> *1/7/08 12:48 a.m. Mood: Tired*
>
> *Today went by sooo slow! Ugh! But Calvin was talking to me and my heart was racing and my neck burning, my palms sweating. I was gonna ask him something but I couldn't do it in front of the class! >.<! At the end of the day, at Carey's, Sam found him on Facebook. Things I learned: He likes scrubs, The Beatles, Kill Bill, Pulp Fiction, and he drinks (not surprising).*

Unfortunately, this digging for information in the dark of night to try to casually bring it up during the day was slow going. After all, I had only a few months! I was impatient and totally in love. I had to make my feelings known. That's how it works in the movies. The characters boldly declare their feelings, find out that they're reciprocated and live happily ever after, with '80s rock playing in the background.

> *1/23/2008 4:23 p.m. Mood: Blushing Shock O_O!*

School, whatever. But at the end of the day, I told Cal...that I liked him. I was going to go down the stairs, guess who shows up? So I turn around. Tap him on the shoulder. I was like, "Hey, Cal. Can I talk to you for a second?" Cal puts his arm around my shoulders and says, "Sure, what's up?" So he leans his neck down and I'm talking with my head up, kind of craned to talk into his ear. Me: "Cal...this is really random and I just thought you should know that...um...I like you." He turns his head and smiles and says, "Thanks!"

Sixteen-year-old me was so confused. Where was the reciprocation? Is thanking me a weird form of dude talk for "I like you, too"? I had walked away feeling proud of my bold actions. I hoped that maybe something would come of it. Maybe it was too sudden and he needed time to process the information. Yes, that seemed likely. Boys weren't used to girls expressing their feelings in such a bold, fearless way. I would give him some space.

By now it was late January. I had less than five months to make him mine, but I was ready. Until...I learned he had a girlfriend. I was stunned. But I convinced myself that high school relationships didn't last, even though I was gunning for the same high-school relationship myself.

1/29/08 Tuesday Mood: _____

So end of midterms. Yay! Cal has a girlfriend and I dunno how to take it. I'm not bothered... at all. O.O I really, really, really like him. But, high school things don't last; so I'm not hoping for him to break up with her or anything. I hope that he's happy. Who knows! Maybe five years from now I'll run into Cal and maybe we'll have something! My heart will always have something for Cal. Maybe he'll break up with her...who knows, right?

As January turned into February, and with Valentine's Day right around the corner, I was hopelessly optimistic. Our school had roses you could buy for a dollar to help fund our dances. My friends had teased me that Cal was going to buy me one. Completely unlikely, considering he had a girlfriend, but that didn't stop me from blushing and being giddy about the idea of it. I made brownies on Valentine's for my Computer Art class, the one class I shared with Calvin. My declaration of my true feelings hadn't worked. Begin Plan of Action B: tempt him with delicious baked goods. I was an expert in boxed brownies. It was on this day, the most romantic of holidays, that Calvin declared his love for me.

2/14/08 Thursday 11:49 p.m. Mood: _____

I made brownies and Cal was like, "Megan, I'm so happy. You bring tears to my eyes." And I went around the room, passed them out. Alex was like, "Will you feed me one?" Me: "What... no...." And Calvin was last, but I went to him and was like, "Last but not least." He took a brownie and said, "I love you." And I was like O_O, "Thanks."

Okay, he didn't really declare his love. But instinctively I knew that saying "I love you" in front of our class had been less a heartfelt expression of his true feelings and more of a joke, really. He was our class clown, after all. I had won the admiration of his stomach instead of his heart.

My Plan of Action B had failed. It was time to revisit Plan of Action A and see if I'd missed anything. I employed my cousin, Samantha, who helped me with my Facebook stalking. Samantha was thrilled. She thought my crush was hilarious and took any opportunity to tease me about it. Once again, instead of behaving like a normal human being and having a conversation with the guy, I researched him like he was an otherworldly specimen. I found out his birthday and compared our zodiac signs. According to the universe, we were compatible. What more proof did I need that we were meant to be together?

Late into February, I discovered that his girlfriend's Facebook profile now said "Single." I had not only scoured Cal's Facebook page for likes, dislikes and so forth, but I had kept tabs on his girlfriend, too. I clearly remember skipping out on my second-period study hall to hang with my best friend, Serena, because she was in woodshop class, and guess who spent his second period in that same woodshop class? Yes. Him. Cal. The boy of my dreams! I didn't have his schedule memorized, but I knew where he might be on certain class rotations. March was beginning and we still weren't dating. What was I doing wrong?

3/26/08 Wednesday Mood: Annoyed!

I've been so busy and so tired! Chorus rehearsals and drama club are killing me. Then...OMFG! I was in the computer lab for class and I saw Cal walking around the library. He saw me thru the glass, I kinda waved, and...he winked at me! Oh, god, I just started smiling. I know it was towards me. Ughhh I can't stop grinning like a fool.

4/11/08 Monday Mood: Tired

I went to a lacrosse game w/ Serena to "babysit" her because she was on pain meds. I saw Cal there. He may have waved to me? IDK :/

4/14/08 Thursday Mood: Hyper + blushing

On Facebook, on Saturday, I wrote on Cal's wall: "I think I saw you at the lacrosse game." Today, he wrote on my wall, "Well, I think I saw you." Now I'm all giggly GAAH!

4/21/08 Thursday 11:35 p.m. Mood: Tired but happy

I IM'd him around 8? We talked till a little after 11 p.m. I was so nervous, my heart was racing. We talked about NIN, movies, Harley motorcycles, directors/actors, being old and how each don't wanna live past 50. We talked about random things, and I quizzed him on movies. It was just a ping-pong of conversations. It was really nice.

I cut my hair, I dyed it, I liked the same music as him, I liked some of the same movies. He never said that he just wanted to be friends. Perhaps, if he had, I would have laid this to rest and not spent nearly two years pining for him.

By May, it was time for Plan of Action C. I had tried tempting him with baked goods, I had done my research, I had listened to the same music, but what I hadn't done was be myself. I had been so caught up in being the type of person Cal would like that I hadn't tried just being me. It was then, I think, that I made the most progress. My diary entries went back to how they were before I met him, no longer dedicated to detailed accounts of our conversations.

> *5/13/08 Tuesday 1:50 p.m. Mood: Fine*
>
> *I got the online fixed and ended up talking to Cal. We had a heart-to-heart and I saw him in a new light. Which was nice.... A lovely quality that Cal has is that he's willing to listen to anyone. I admire that.*

I finally stopped trying so hard to be this other person. I realized that no one is going to fall in love with someone you're not. God, why would I have wanted him to? I would have needed to be this pretend person for who knows how long. I would have been miserable. Our actual friendship developed, but did I still have romantic feelings for him? Yes. Putting those romantic feelings aside, did I genuinely care about him as a fellow human being? Yes.

> *5/19/08 Monday 10:08 p.m. Mood: Very happy*
>
> *At 9:24 p.m., Cal IM'd me. It made my heart race.... We're talking about NIN 'cause he's writing a paper on Trent Reznor. I'm giving him ideas and he said, "I'm very happy to be talking to you right now." It made me blush wildly.*

During the month of May—yes, with one month left until graduation—I had a miserable virus. I was out of school for days. In my fevered state, I realized that I should probably just start telling people I loved them. When I returned to school, I began saying to people, "You're a beautiful person and I love you."

> *5/20/08 Tuesday 9:30 p.m. Mood: Sick but content*
>
> *At the moment, I'm sipping hot cocoa, blowing my nose, talking to Sam + Cal. I read a book about Karma today. It truly opened my eyes and now I am going to try and think no more negative thoughts and send my love to everyone!*
>
> *5/21/08 Wednesday 10:52 p.m. Mood: Alright*
>
> *Still sick and no voice. Blech :(Cal let me read his NIN paper + I showed him my Ghost CD. Then, I was outside with Serena and I was telling everyone today that I loved them. I really shouldn't talk but I'm hoping I'll be fixed (lol).*

It was June when I told Cal that I'd miss him. It was true, and some part of my 16-year-old brain was clinging to the idea that maybe if I just blurted out my feelings all the time then something would happen. I had to take part in the graduation ceremony because I was a member of our school choir. In the stifling heat of our gym, I didn't have any butterflies in my stomach nor did my heart race upon seeing the object of my affection. Afterward, I gave him a CD of some songs I wanted him to listen to, and he gave me a hug.

6/19/08 Thursday 11:43 a.m. Mood: ____

I think, mentally, seeing him in his gown and cap, finally put him out of my reach. I accepted that I think a part of me still wants to be friends and that's okay. I'm glad I'm not hurting. I'm proud of him! Saturday and Friday I'm gonna hang out with Ashley! We're going bowling!! :D

That would be where the story ends, right? On a nice, happy note. But it doesn't exactly end there. Throughout my junior year of high school, I still held some strange infatuation with him. I saw him from time to time, and the endorphins kicked in each freaking time.

8/26/08 Tuesday 9:11 p.m. Mood: Excited

Cal IM'd me last night and said, "Good luck junior year, Megan." He even said, "Talk to you sooner than later." Ugh, boys! So troublesome. It was so out of the blue, like whoaah! Hello!

> *8/28/08 Thursday 8:25 p.m. Mood: Thoughtful*
>
> *I saw Calvin at school! He walked by my class. My heart jumped. Then raced. Then my hands began to shake. "WTF?" my mind thought with racing speed. I didn't see him again that day. I'm so confused. I didn't think I'd see him again.*

Eventually, I saw him less and less and talked to him less and less. It was a gradual decaying of love. The last diary entry that mentions Calvin was eight months later.

> *4/20/09 5:41 p.m. Mood: Contemplative (omg, big words!)*
>
> *I haven't talked to Calvin in forever. But, I saw him @ the variety show a while back. The week before vacation I saw him when he came into my English class. We waved.*

Even though it's embarrassing to flip through those glitter-penned pages of my diary, I'm glad to have felt what I did. This unreciprocated love of mine is how I learned to be bold, take risks and try to be less creepy. Seriously, 16-year-old me, Facebook stalking is not how you get a boyfriend. In this chaotic mess of a life, just because your star signs line up doesn't mean the universe wants you to be together. No matter how good your brownies are.

 **Megan Arnold** *has blue hair. That is a very important detail that you should know. At least, it was blue at the time this picture was taken. She lives in Enfield, Connecticut. It's a small town with cows and lots of tobacco fields. As you might imagine, it's not the most exciting place to live. Writing had always been her personal, secret door to another time and place. "384 Days" is her first story to be published, but certainly not her last.*

SAFE DUTY ASSIGNMENT

Thomas Johnson

WITH A FIFTH OF JACK DANIELS and another of Wild Turkey in my oversized pants pockets designed for carrying ammo—and a special surprise in a brown paper bag—I headed for the red-light district of Can Tho. If you were dressed as an American soldier in olive drab and extending a thumb, someone on a little Honda would pick you up for a dollar then take you anywhere in the city.

That hot humid morning, I jumped off the bike and walked toward my girl's apartment, breathing in the usual smell of rotting food. This time, a large potbelly pig and several chickens rooted through garbage placed on the side of the wide street, all crumbling asphalt and dirt with deep potholes filled with stinky muddy water. Three children were herding quacking ducks to the river. As I walked, the aroma of street vendors cooking spicy Vietnamese food and baking bread replaced the stench.

People crossed the street from any point they chose with little regard to motor traffic, which would come from any direction. Scooters flashed by with beautiful young women in white clothing hanging on for dear life to young Vietnamese soldiers. Their putt-putt drowned out most other sounds. The sky was bluer than blue, with giant, scurrying white clouds so low they seemed just out of reach.

Two doors away from her apartment, I saw Hoa crossing the street. She wore a tiny white sleeveless dress hemmed about two inches above her slightly bowed knees, showing ivory legs with just a hint of calf muscle. Through her thin cotton dress, in the sunlight, her golden nipples could be seen on small motionless unsupported breasts. Her silken raven-black hair falling to her hips was loose. Tiny tan leather flip-flops with silver studs adorned beautiful little red-pedicured feet. Four feet 10 inches tall and 90 pounds of Chinese-Vietnamese princess, Can Tho royalty. She carried herself as if floating across the dusty street, a precious stone on a sandy beach. She had very little hips and no booty to speak of, but there was a lot of motion under that dress. Amazing. The song "Backfield in Motion" always came to mind. I'm gonna have to penalize you.

I quickened my pace to approach her from behind. I softly called her name, "Hoa"—Vietnamese for flower or blossom.

Hoa nonchalantly looked over her shoulder without stopping and said in perfect non-accented English,

"Oh my God!" We usually communicated by using a gutter mixture of slang Vietnamese, slang English and French, but she was eager to learn actual English. Before I could say another word, she executed a one-eighty and walked past me, head down. She waved at the ground behind her, the signal to follow. Nice young ladies never walked or talked to GIs in public. I followed her back to her apartment building.

As soon as we passed the threshold and its steel door, she took my hand and led me the few steps away so others couldn't see us, turned slowly around, placed my right hand around her waist and looked up at me. "You funny GI. Why you come now?"

"I want to see you now," I said, sweat dripping down my face. Hoa always had a pleasant, cool moistness even on the most humid of days; she never perspired. "I have whiskey for you." I never knew how much she got for selling American booze and cigarettes on the black market, but I do know it made her very happy to get them.

She looked down at my pockets and smiled. "You number one GI. You number one for me all time. Come, we di-di." *Hurry up.* She took my hand and we marched up the three flights of stairs (no elevator) to her one-room apartment.

The stairs spiraled up the center of the three-story building to the roof. Rooms on each floor opened to the staircase. The voices of adults and the cries of babies echoed off the plastered walls. A hallway did not exist in that narrow apartment house. When the ground floor doors were opened and the huge skylight was raised, hot air rose up, bringing cooler air from the ground floor and creating a wind tunnel up the spiral staircase. Doors on the third floor were often kept open for the breeze.

Hoa opened her unlocked door, then turned around and shouted something in Vietnamese down the staircase. We walked into the small 15-by-20 box of a room that had one window and one door. A queen-sized bed sat under the window with Playboy Playmates for 1968 on the wall where the headboard would usually be. The bathroom/shower was shared by all on the third floor. Hoa turned on the two large fans, then spoke to a young girl who came in. Hoa hired the girl to iron her clothes with the steam iron I had bought her a week prior. I awkwardly stood next to the large bed while they spoke, cooing back and forth like mourning doves.

I placed the bag on the bed and took the Wild Turkey out of my pocket. Hoa took out the other bottle, and I handed her the Turkey.

"You number one for me, Pineapple." My name, Thom, translated into Vietnamese is pineapple, and she thought it endearing and witty to use the English translation. She placed the bottles on her Victorian-style steamer trunk, then came back and pushed me playfully down on the bed as she had done in the past. She jumped on next to me, crossed her legs, bounced up and down happily. I took a box out of the bag and handed her the gift of Kotex.

She whispered, "Oh my God." Her exotic almond eyes teared up. Soon black eyeliner ran down her alabaster cheeks. Her pink lips quivered.

Hoa reverently placed her gift—and the bottles—inside the trunk, a little wrinkle between her eyebrows as if she were in deep thought, then came back to put both feet in my lap. She took my hand and placed it on a cute little foot and gently gave my hand a squeeze, encouraging me to massage her perfect lovely toes. Even the little toe was flawless. Since kissing was rare in South East Asia, we touched like this often.

She looked down at my hand on her soft foot, then said, "You love me *beaucoup*. I never know GI love me same-same you. You number one for me for sure." She looked into my eyes, with mascara staining her cheeks, then suddenly pushed me over to take my wallet out of my hip pocket. She took out $20 then gave the wallet back. "I go work now. You give Mama-san money, we come back. I love you long time."

"You go work, I stay. I go sleep two, maybe three hours."

"No! You di-di same-same me. We talk Mama-san. You give money, I sleep with you. Get up! Di-di!"

I followed her at a respectful distance to the White Horse Bar and took a seat in the same booth I had met Hoa in three months earlier. She worked as a Saigon tea girl.

The White Horse, a respectable bar, served drinks and Vietnamese sandwiches to GIs. The place was well-lit with Asian ambiance, gave off the spicy aroma of incense and had framed pictures of dragons on the walls. A large fat smiling Buddha greeted you at the door, and a lovely tea girl would escort the GI to one of the large vinyl-covered booths, then sit down with him to take his order and get a Saigon Tea (Kool-Aid) for herself.

Hoa came over and sat in my lap, then put her arm around my shoulders to whisper in my ear, "You buy me tea, I talk to Mama-san." She kissed my ear, then jumped up to get my usual—an American Pabst Blue Ribbon beer—and her tea.

Mama-san, a very attractive 30ish light-brown woman, rushed from the back to the front door talking rapidly to the tea girls. Hoa jumped off my lap and said something to the other girls, then moved to the booth seat facing me and watched Mama-san at the door as if expecting instructions.

A masculine voice outside spoke Vietnamese loudly. A young man with wild-looking eyes as if he were on uppers and wearing all black confidently walked up to Mama-san, talking rapidly. Mama-san took the man by the arm and led him to the small counter. He sat on a stool while she spoke to him.

Hoa said, "No look him eye, Pineapple. He bad man. He number 10." Number one or number 10—nothing in between.

She didn't have to tell me twice. I stared down at my can of Pabst, and she did the same with her little shot glass of Kool-Aid. We must have looked like we were saying grace over our drinks.

Mama-san began chirping. Hoa and the other girls talked all at the same time while moving toward Mama-san and the wild-eyed guy in uniform.

Hoa said, "You di-di, Pineapple. Not good here."

"I'll wait for you at your place."

She stood over me and hit me in the chest with her fist. "No! You go back airfield." Then in a quieter voice she said, "Come back tomorrow." She reached for my watch and pointed to the three. "How you say, tree?" I nodded. "You come back tree tomorrow. Pineapple, no be stupid. Di-di now, got damn, di-di!"

She scared the shit out of me. She never cursed before, not in English anyway. I briskly walked out as Hoa moved toward Mama-san and the crazy guy. I wanted to tell her I had to work tomorrow all day, but I didn't want to be stupid.

At the main road, after about three minutes of hitchhiking, a U.S. Army truck picked me up. I joined two other GIs in the back going to the airfield. Before I got seated, a loud explosion from the road in front of us knocked me to the floor. The truck driver informed us a South Vietnamese Army jeep had just blown up and the driver was on the road, not moving. From the back of the large deuce-and-a-half truck, we couldn't see until we drove around the jeep's axle and saw the smoking wreckage in the ditch. The South Vietnamese soldier was sitting in the road with both legs out in front, his upper body leaning forward, arms at his sides like a rag doll, unmoving. The driver increased his speed to get away from any further danger.

I made it to the sanctuary of the airfield, shaking. What was going on? A bad-looking Vietnamese man, perhaps VC, and a deadly explosion. Has the war come to Can Tho? I crawled onto my bunk with my boots on, not where I had planned to sleep that morning.

Richard Kennedy woke me. "Where's your helmet, dude?"

I opened my eyes and jumped up, thinking I was late for guard duty, before I realized I had been on guard duty 24 hours before that. "What are you doing, Rich? Why is it so dark in here? Turn on the lights." I was confused.

"We're getting hit, man," he said, grinning as he pulled my helmet out of my locker and handed it to me. "The airfield's taking incoming, man. Get your weapon. Sergeant Will sent me to wake you up. We're in the bunker. Di-di, man, move out!"

The communications team bunker was a large Tuff Shed-like building with green sandbags all around it and on the flat roof. Four beams inside reinforced the weight of the ceiling. A gas generator out back powered the beer-filled refrigerator, fans and lights. Swirling smoke from marijuana, opium and cigarettes gave the bunker a ghostly atmosphere in the low light. Cots were provided for those who needed sleep.

In the middle of this spacious bunker, Sergeant Will Sanders and three others were playing Tonk for money. Tonk was a southern card game he had introduced to us signal guys. "How's it hangin', lover man?"

"Someone tell me what's happening."

Will answered while studying his cards. "The Viet Cong are firing rockets at the airfield. My man Tricky Dicky Nixon has pissed them off big time. Right on! You gotta love it."

I sat on a couple of sandbags against a wall. I was hungry, but only beer would be in the box. I picked up a C-ration.

Will was holding court. "Lyons, you a religious man?"

"I guess. Why?" Lyons asked, rearranging cards in his hand.

"Evolution is in the Bible. Everyone listen up. In Genesis, every day that God created something, it was better than the day before. Right? God created man, then he created woman. Woman, therefore, is more evolved than man. Did you all hear me?" No reply from any of us to this daily reported revelation. But I was rapidly becoming a convert.

After the rocket attack on the airfield, we were restricted to base for two weeks. I was going through

Hoa withdrawal, worried about that strange guy and her behavior. As soon as I could get away, I made it to the White Horse Tea Bar and received my "Oh my God!" greeting. We continued where we left off last time. I gave Mama-san $30 (the amount Hoa would have made that day, with a little extra) and spent the day and night with her. We never spoke of the mystery man.

The next month, I was with Hoa about three days a week, and on one visit—after she cooked a duck on her electric hot plate/wok on the floor (she could squat like a two-year old for hours) for dinner—we were playing around (she loved to ride on my back horsey-style) when I stopped and asked her, "Would you like to come to America?"

Her smile went away. Her pupils were invisible, her dark eyes suspended in pure white. After a long pregnant pause, she spoke softly. "You stupid GI, Pineapple. Why you be stupid to me?" She was getting louder, and those eyes were beginning to drown in tears. "I no go America. I go America, you see America girl." She pointed at the Playboy centerfolds over her bed. She pointed to Miss May's breast. "America girl!" She screamed. She unbuttoned her blouse to expose her perfect rock-solid B-cup breast. "This Hoa! I number 10!" She waved up and down over her body. "Where I go when you go be with got damn round-eye America girl? I no stupid, Pineapple!" She was full-blown crying and yelling. Her eyes were melting, dripping black from her tiny chin.

"Hold on, Hoa. I'll never leave you. I didn't mean…. American girl no look like that, Hoa. I like the way you look. American girl same-same you." She was breathing hard and crying very loudly. "You *beaucoup dap*….*beaucoup dap*, Hoa. You very beautiful." I wanted to hold her but knew better.

"You lie! You go! You no come back!" she screamed, pounding on my chest as hard as she could, scaring the shit out of me again.

I backed up in a circle trying to get away from her. "Hoa! I can't go. It's after curfew time."

"You go! Got damn you, stupid!" She stopped. She stood with arms down, hands fisted, the fan blowing her long raven hair and blouse up and away from her body, nipples and lips forming three points of matching pink against her pale white flawless body, her eyes dripping black. I felt panic overtaking me. I didn't know what she might do next, or who might come in to help her kick me out. I figured it would be better to take my chances with the MPs that patrolled the streets after eight o'clock.

As I ran down the stairs, every door was open, with familiar faces gawking grimly at me. As I reached the dark street, I could still hear, over the hammering of my heart, Hoa wailing.

I traveled 50 yards toward the main road when my man with the little motorcycle pulled up and took me to the closed airfield gate. While I was giving him a generous tip, a deuce-and-a-half Army truck pulled up, and the gate opened. I walked in on the opposite side from where the guard stood. I was very lucky that night.

I stayed away for six weeks. Maybe Hoa was some kind of psycho and couldn't help it, I said to myself as I replayed that night over and over. But I also promised myself it was over. She knew GIs had been killed and robbed after curfew. She didn't care about me, I thought.

At the end of the six weeks, I couldn't take it any longer. I had suffered Hoa withdrawal long enough. I worked a half-day and took off to the White Horse Tea Bar. I looked around for Hoa but didn't see her.

Mama-san came over. "Pineapple, long time no see you."

"Where is Hoa, Mama-san?"

"I have new girl," she said while calling a very pretty young French/Vietnamese girl over. "She number one for you."

"Thank you, Mama-san. She *beaucoup dap*. Is Hoa here?"

"Pineapple, Hoa no work here. You buy tea for new girl. She say you dap."

"Where Hoa go?" I asked loudly.

"Okay, I know you long time. You good GI. Hoa good girl. Hoa work American Eagle Club."

I knew the American Eagle. It was a big club in downtown Can Tho that served American food and drinks to mostly U.S. officers and lifers. It also had live entertainment until curfew most nights and was considered a high-end club, on par with clubs in Saigon.

I jumped on a motorcycle rickshaw taxi to the American Eagle. The club was on the bottom floor of a three-story French Colonial–style building. The building was leased by the U.S. government, which occupied the other two floors for Army Administration functions.

The club had a high spacious ceiling with American ambiance. Flags from all 50 states hung down over the customers. Posters of sports stars adorned the walls, along with American muscle cars—Mustangs, Camaros and Indy cars. The jukebox played Elvis Presley songs. Hamburgers and New York steaks were served by young women in the traditional Vietnamese dress of loose satin pants with silk sleeveless garments that fit firmly on top then flowed to the knees, front and back, in two parts of semi-transparent silk. The girls wore the same outfits with different color combinations, and all had long hair gathered into glossy fishtail braids that flowed to the butt.

The club also provided a gym and massage, along with manicures given by 10-year-old girls who moved from booth to booth carrying tiny cases, peddling their skill. A lot of the married GIs took advantage of the massage with "you want happy end," or better known as a steam-and-cream, with some guys scheduling regular appointments. For more intimacy, next door was the

Green Door with dozens of attractive girls to choose from who were tested weekly by U.S. doctors to make sure they were clean and healthy.

The girls in the club would bring food and drink to the military customers—American, Australian, Canadian, South Korean and Thai soldiers. Civilian contractors from who knows where were large in numbers. Each girl sat with a customer and engaged in small talk, or not, depending on the patron's mood.

I was approached by a beautiful girl who wore traditional Indian dress, similar to the Vietnamese dress except she had a pattern of tiny pink flowers on her outfit and a red dot on her forehead. She was the hostess/manager. "Welcome," she said in perfect British-accented English. "How many?"

"Just me. May I sit at the counter?"

"Yes, of course. Do you have a favorite girl to take your order?"

Taken aback, I said, possibly too loudly, "Hoa."

"Sir, we have several young ladies by that name. Do you see her?"

I did, sitting with a group of five officers and three girls in a large booth in the center of the large hall. "She's sitting there." I nodded in the direction. "Next to the Major."

"Would you like to wait for her?"

"Yes, thank you."

"Sir, please order a drink from Danny while you wait. I'll let Hoa know you are here."

She floated over to where Hoa was seated and spoke to her. Hoa looked at me, and her face changed from serious to a shy blushing smile. I was relieved and felt a new fondness for her. She spoke at length to the hostess.

The lovely hostess returned. "My name is Sharmila. Hoa tells me that you are a very special friend and that she is happy to see you. She wants me to tell you that she will complete her shift at six o'clock. Hoa would like you to meet her at her apartment."

I thanked her, finished my beer and walked out without looking back, while Charley Pride sang "All I Have to Offer You (Is Me)." I felt great.

I had about two hours to stroll the beautiful French-Colonial city with its huge tropical trees, lovely parks and busy marketplace. I stood outside at the front door of the building, wondering if I should bring up that the war would be over soon and that she could visit me in California. If she didn't like it, I would send her home. All the Americans knew we would win the war and all would be peaceful. Best to not bring it up this visit.

Danny, the bartender, drove up to the apartment house with two girls on the back of his Suzuki. Hoa got off gracefully and very coolly took my hand and led me into the building where we embraced like we had so many times before. She kissed me on the mouth, something she rarely did but something I always tried to encourage. I took it as a welcome-back gesture, or perhaps she was forgiving me for being so naive. Without speaking, she took my hand and we trotted up the three flights of stairs.

The door was open. The young girl was ironing clothes on a board on the floor in the hot room with both fans blowing. Hoa looked up at me with new eyes, no longer ringed only in black mascara. Now, she had her eyelids shaded in a light green that matched her top. The liner under her eyes extended longer than it had before, creating a lovely exotic Asian look. Her eyebrows were thinner and longer, too.

"You look beautiful," I said. "*Beaucoup dap*, Hoa."

"Thank you. You look for me at American Eagle? Why you no come for me long time, Pineapple?" she said demurely, looking down at my boots as I held her close by the waist.

"I made you mad at me."

She turned to the girl and spoke to her while moving to her steamer chest. The girl answered but continued to work. Hoa opened the chest and gracefully squatted down and began to move items around. She took something out and came back over to where I stood in the middle of the room.

"Have a seat," she said, leading me over to the bed and pushing me down playfully.

"Hoa, you speak English good."

"I go to English school now. You will help me talk English, okay?" she said, standing over me with smiling eyes and holding a little box.

"Good for you. Yes, I will help you with English." I nodded at the box. "What's that?"

She pulled out a gold chain with a little ivory Buddha hanging from it. "You been away long time. Are you a butterfly now?" she asked me, with daggers in her eyes.

A "butterfly" is a GI who has many girlfriends, like a butterfly sticking his nose in all the pretty flowers. Nice girls are very concerned about illnesses spread by the GI butterfly.

"No. I number one for you. Always and forever."

She placed the Buddha around my neck and kissed me on the neck. She also gave me several professional pictures of herself in different poses to be placed in my wallet, then she jumped into my lap, laughing and hugging until I rolled over on my back. She was happy. I was now a marked man. No other girl would ever talk to me with Buddha near my heart and pictures of Hoa near my money.

"I can sing song for you." She started to sing, in the sweetest little voice, "One little, two little, three little Indians." Then she and the girl started in on "Ballin' the Jack," in perfect harmony.

"You are very smart to learn so much English so fast," I said, very proud of her.

She sat up. "What state are you from? How long have you been in Vietnam? May I get something for you?" She had to be able to speak English small talk to be successful at her new job. She was going to be good.

She held my hand. "You stay long time?"

"No. Not tonight. I'll come back in two days and stay long time."

"Okay." She smiled, speaking slowly. "You come back on, how you say, Thursday?"

"Yes. I'll be back Thursday after your work." I stood up. "I better go, it's getting late." Nice young ladies who have male visitors for a short visit will always have someone else in the room. If I were to stay the night, the young girl would have been asked to leave. No "quickies."

At the door, I reached into my big shirt pocket and pulled out a pale green jade bracelet I had ordered a month ago from the Japanese PX catalog. I held it up for her to see. Her eyes pooled with tears. "Oh my God!" Then Hoa spoke quickly to the young girl, asking her to bring something to remove her makeup. After Hoa had wiped the makeup off, she put her tiny hand through the little bracelet, then jumped into my arms and wept for three minutes onto my shirt. I held her little body lovingly.

That Thursday morning, after guard duty, the first sergeant came in and told all of us that the U.S. military was pulling out of Can Tho, Vietnam, ASAP. Nixon's plan to have the South Vietnamese Army gradually take over was to begin in the area south of Saigon, Can Tho, the provincial capital. The first sergeant passed out our new orders. Mike Russo and I were to report to Cam Ranh Bay the very next day.

I was frantic. I had to get a message to Hoa to let her know I was leaving and that I would return for her. But how do I do that? What's her last name? What's her address? Is there even a phone at the apartment building? Perhaps, I thought, I could get the address and phone for the American Eagle.

But The American Eagle was already closed. Hoa no longer had a job. Where would she go? I had just three letters: H, O and A. Her name was more common than Mary.

That was it. Not meant to be. Two ships passing on a peaceful sea, clear sky in bright sunlight, moving toward opposite horizons, happy to see one another for a few hours but never to meet again.

It hurt a lot and took more time than I realized it would to get over. Now, looking back, I hope she is safe and has had a good life. I still think of her.

**Thomas Johnson** *grew up in south-central Los Angeles so long ago it was nice. In high school he looked and behaved like Steve Urkel from the TV show, bugging all the pretty girls. Three years in the Army—with one year in Vietnam—changed him from Urkel into GI Joe. Thomas returned home and got a job, married his sister's best friend and finished college with a BA in psychology. He and his wife raised two daughters and now have three grandkids, a girl and two boys. After 33 years with AT&T as a fiber optic cable tester, Thomas is retired. He has two short stories in print and one Internet-online story.*

*Would you like to learn
more about our authors?*

*Do you want to buy
a book for a friend?*

Are you just plain nosy?

Visit us at
WWW.DAMMITBOOK.COM

www.ingramcontent.com/pod-product-compliance
Lightning Source LLC
Chambersburg PA
CBHW050634300426
44112CB00012B/1787